*Study Guide
for*

Conlin's

The American Past

A SURVEY OF AMERICAN HISTORY

VOLUME II: SINCE 1865

Seventh Edition

Brian Gordon
St. Louis Community College at Florissant Valley

THOMSON
WADSWORTH

Australia • Canada • Mexico • Singapore • Spain • United Kingdom • United States

COPYRIGHT © 2004 Wadsworth, a division of Thomson Learning, Inc. Thomson Learning™ is a trademark used herein under license.

ALL RIGHTS RESERVED. No part of this work covered by the copyright hereon may be reproduced or used in any form or by any means—graphic, electronic, or mechanical, including but not limited to photocopying, recording, taping, Web distribution, information networks, or information storage and retrieval systems—without the written permission of the publisher.

Printed in the United States of America
1 2 3 4 5 6 7 07 06 05 04 03

Printer: Globus Printing

ISBN: 0-534-62141-4

For more information about our products, contact us at:
Thomson Learning Academic Resource Center
1-800-423-0563

For permission to use material from this text, contact us by:
Phone: 1-800-730-2214
Fax: 1-800-730-2215
Web: http://www.thomsonrights.com

Cover image: Getty Images; *New Beginnings,* circa 1915

Wadsworth/Thomson Learning
10 Davis Drive
Belmont, CA 94002-3098
USA

Asia
Thomson Learning
5 Shenton Way #01-01
UIC Building
Singapore 068808

Australia/New Zealand
Thomson Learning
102 Dodds Street
Southbank, Victoria 3006
Australia

Canada
Nelson
1120 Birchmount Road
Toronto, Ontario M1K 5G4
Canada

Europe/Middle East/South Africa
Thomson Learning
High Holborn House
50/51 Bedford Row
London WC1R 4LR
United Kingdom

Latin America
Thomson Learning
Seneca, 53
Colonia Polanco
11560 Mexico D.F.
Mexico

Spain/Portugal
Paraninfo
Calle/Magallanes, 25
28015 Madrid, Spain

Table of Contents

To The Instructor

To The Student

Chapter 25	Aftermath	181
Chapter 26	Parties, Patronage, and Pork	189
Chapter 27	Big Industry, Big Business	198
Chapter 28	Living with Leviathan	206
Chapter 29	We Who Built America	214
Chapter 30	Bright Lights and Slums	222
Chapter 31	The Last Frontier	229
Chapter 32	Stressful Times Down Home	237
Chapter 33	In the Days of McKinley	245
Chapter 34	Theodore Roosevelt and the Good Old Days	254
Chapter 35	Age of Reform	262
Chapter 36	Standing at Armageddon	271
Chapter 37	Over There	279
Chapter 38	Over Here	288
Chapter 39	The Days of Harding	296
Chapter 40	Calvin Coolidge and the New Era	305
Chapter 41	National Trauma	313
Chapter 42	Rearranging America	321
Chapter 43	Another Great War	330
Chapter 44	Fighting World War II	339

Chapter 45	Cold War	348
Chapter 46	Eisenhower Country	357
Chapter 47	Ike and Camelot	365
Chapter 48	Johnson's Great Society	374
Chapter 49	Presidency in Crisis	383
Chapter 50	Morning in America	392
Chapter 51	The Millennium Years	399

To the Instructor

This study guide is intended to supplement Joseph R. Conlin's *The American Past*, Seventh Edition, as a resource for teaching and learning the history of the United States. It is designed to allow you and your students considerable flexibility in its use; whether your style of teaching emphasizes individual study or classroom/small group discussions, the study questions and exercises for each chapter of *The American Past* can be adapted to your needs.

A common lament among many teachers of history is that today's young students *just don't know anything*. That this complaint has been made in every generation is both true and irrelevant to the instructor who is trying to get classroom discussion going among students who have no knowledge of the past and therefore no historical frame of reference. Whether the ignorance of Generation X (or Y or Z) is any worse than that of students of any earlier time is a judgment usually made without persuasive evidence. Much of the problem is of course simply generational. Many historians regard the Vietnam War, for example, as one of the significant events of contemporary U.S. history—their generation's war, whether or not they had a personal involvement in that conflict. But for increasing numbers of today's students, Vietnam is not only not their war, it is not even a war their fathers fought (or avoided)—it is fast becoming their *grandfather's* war. (The U.S. entry into the Vietnam War is now as far removed from students in the new millennium as the start of the Civil War was from Americans at the beginning of the 20th century.)

Educators debate whether it is best to emphasize the accumulation of facts or to concentrate on the analysis of facts, as if one approach were possible without the other. Rote memorization of facts—names, dates, treaties, laws, statistics—is of course a time-honored method of teaching history, whether or not students learn anything of lasting value from these test-oriented rituals of memorization. Testing factual knowledge is easy, of course; there is an appearance of precision in dates and names, compared to the fuzziness of subjective questions. But memorization can easily become an end in itself, and is one reason so many students dread having to take history courses.

At the other end of the spectrum is the view that holds all historical "facts" to be suspect, the arbitrary result of power relationships in society, determined by economic status, race, gender, social class or other immutable conditions. Often using terms like "critical thinking" or "empowerment," followers of this theory of education tend to have students engage in group projects and collaborative activities—process more than content. But if classroom discussions of history are to be productive and effective, students must have a working knowledge of the basic vocabulary of history. Absent a common understanding of the major historical events of the past, student discussions will be nothing more than circles of ignorance in which strongly held but entirely unsupported feelings about the past masquerade as truth, and all opinions, however far-fetched, will seem equally valid.

There is no substitute for a common vocabulary in any field of study. History is no different in this regard than any other discipline—most of what we consider to be knowledge is simply the appropriate terminology understood in relation to its particular context. To the student who remembers little from his or her previous history courses, the difference between information essential to the understanding of history, compared to the trivial or merely illustrative, is of course not always obvious—*all* the information may seem equally irrelevant.

This study guide encourages students first to learn the basic vocabulary of United States history, either by study alone or in the context of a classroom or small-group collaboration. Each chapter in this study guide begins with a list of key words from the text, the understanding of which is essential before students can productively engage in informed discussion, analysis or critical thinking about the people, ideas and events discussed in the chapter. True-false, multiple-choice, fill-in and essay questions allow students to self-test their understanding of the reading assignments. There is no single way you and your students should use this study guide. You may wish to add or delete specific questions or types of questions to fit your own approach to teaching history. Answers to all the questions except for the essay topics are found in the back of each chapter, so this study guide is not intended to serve as a test bank. Also—particularly in the case of the fill-in questions—the information required to answer the questions is probably more specific and detailed than most instructors would expect their students to be able to recite from memory. The intent of the detailed statistical fill-in answers is to illustrate historical trends and changes over time and to focus students' attention in a more precise way than would be true if language less specific were to be used.

Brian Gordon

To the Student: How to Use This Study Guide

This study guide has many uses. First, of course, it supplements the Seventh Edition of Joseph R. Conlin's textbook, *The American Past: A Survey of American History*. This particular textbook is especially rich in descriptive information and interesting, often unusual and fascinating data. As is true for most history textbooks, *The American Past* is a narrative account of United States history, with the story usually told in chronological order within each chapter. The chapters themselves are arranged overall in a chronological order, although specific chapters will examine broad topical themes within a historical period. Your instructor will probably assign chapters to be read in the same order as they appear in the text. Whether your instructor follows the author's chapter sequence or not, each chapter in this study guide can stand alone. It is not necessary to have read previous chapters in the text or study guide in order to make sense of the questions found in each chapter of this study guide.

Each chapter in this study guide begins with a list of key words or phrases that can be found in the corresponding chapter of the Conlin textbook. Some of these keywords may be repeated from earlier chapters, but are included both for emphasis and in case the earlier chapter or chapters have not yet been assigned. The determination of what is considered a "key word" is of course subjective; your instructor may wish to add or subtract from the list of key words shown for each chapter.

You will note that not every name, concept, law, or historical event mentioned in the text appears in the key words list. The absence of a word from the key word list does not mean the person, event, law (etc.) is unimportant, and the intent of the list is not to limit your study or your instructor's freedom to emphasize other information in the chapter; rather, it is to help you separate the essential, "must-know" information from the "nice-to-know," less essential details. A beginning student cannot be expected to know the most significant facts about the past—*all* the names may seem equally important (or unimportant), but with practice, you will develop the ability to distinguish between the essential and the peripheral details of history. For example, the winning candidates in a presidential election will always be considered key words, but the losing candidate or candidates may be left off the list, depending on the time period and how important that particular election was. (Recent elections will include both winners and losers; as a rule, chapters covering more recent historical periods have longer key word lists.)

Key words represent the minimum level of knowledge about a historical period. You can consider these to be the brick-and-mortar level of historical knowledge, without which you cannot build a sound structure of interpretation. An interpretation of the past is what historians provide, using specific facts and other details from the past. Interpretation without facts is merely opinion, and one opinion may seem as valid as any other unless it is understood that opinion and judgment must be supported by facts. Therefore, the starting point for an understanding of history is the basic vocabulary of the discipline; that vocabulary, for each period of United States history, is found in the key words list.

Having read the chapter in your text, you should be able, at a minimum, to explain the meaning of each key word. Nearly always, the text will explain a term clearly enough for you to be able to define it, if you are asked. A dictionary or other historical reference book may also help you define each key word. An average student will be able (perhaps simply on the basis of rote memorization) to learn the definitions of a list of key words or phrases. Your goal, however, ought to be to go beyond this minimum level of mastery to reach the next level of accomplishment, which is to be able to explain the historical significance of each word or phrase. In other words, how does the word fit into the broader context of American history? How is the person, event, law or concept related to others? Is there a cause-and-effect relationship among key words in a chapter? Why is the key word important?

The goal here is not simply to commit key words and their definitions to memory, but to understand their relationships to other key words and to the evolution of the history of the United States. The mark of a superior student is the ability to find patterns, connections, cause-and-effect or other relationships among the details of history. Critical analysis of the information learned is essential, and rote memorization will not suffice. The outstanding student will be able to take seemingly unconnected facts about the past and weave them into a seamless tapestry of understanding.

The study guide organizes material in several ways in order to encourage that kind of understanding of history. Several kinds of questions follow the list of key words. The hope is that you will test yourself as you read each chapter in the textbook, keeping in mind always that the goal is not simply the memorization of word meanings—the minimum, least sophisticated measure of learning—but rather the larger goal of critical analysis and historical understanding. To that end, the list of key words is followed by true-false questions, multiple-choice, fill-in, and essay questions. The emphasis is on thinking about the facts, not just memorizing them.

In each category of question, significant pieces of the historical puzzle—information that you will probably find on a test—will appear. Your instructor may have you skip some kinds of questions, depending on his or her teaching style. Some instructors, for example, never use true-false questions, since a student who has done no preparation can guess the right answer 50% of the time. In this study guide, you are to make the false statements correct by changing the faulty part of the statement; merely guessing the right answer isn't enough. (Note that many of the true-false questions are partially true, but include false information as well—be careful!) When you have to change a false statement to make it true, you will learn more than if you can simply mark the answers and move on.

To use this study guide to the best advantage you should read the text carefully before doing the exercises. As you work on the questions, remember that the purpose of these self-testing exercises is to measure your knowledge *before* your instructor gives you a quiz or exam to accomplish the same goal. Work through the questions without looking up the correct answers, which can be found in the back of each chapter. If you get the answers right, then you know you are studying effectively and will probably have no problems with your instructor's exams. But if you cannot answer the questions without looking up the answers, you have an early warning that you need to study more thoroughly. You can then go back to the text and try again.

Quantification has become a vital tool for the historian. Numbers offer more precision than words like "some," "many," "a few," "a handful" or other imprecise terms often used by inexperienced writers. The fill-in questions in particular will require you to look up and write in specific numbers, percentages, dollar amounts, or other data. Here, the intent is to emphasize trends in history, not to force you to memorize statistics for their own sake. You will probably have to look up the information in the text, (and there is a pretty good chance your instructor will also). But statistics have become essential for understanding nearly every historical topic related to economic or demographic change. Therefore, a special section of each chapter is devoted to statistical data from each textbook chapter. These questions require you to fill in blanks with the correct numbers or other information. Such statistical data can be a helpful way to understand a topic; without relevant statistical data, knowledge of a subject remains vague and incomplete. Fill-in questions require you to provide information rather than simply recognize it when presented to you among several other choices. The ability to recall details is a better measure of historical knowledge than simple recognition, though both are useful skills. Your instructor will probably not require you to memorize for examination purposes the specific statistics found in the fill-in questions, but the point of asking you to fill in what might seem to be trivial information is to make a point about the larger issues addressed by the statistics. Note, for example, if a population trend or economic statistic is going up or down as you fill in the information. (You will find that the information needed to answer the fill-in questions will appear in the text in the same order that the questions are found in this study guide.)

Most professors include essay questions on tests. Each chapter in this study guide offers several examples of essay questions, each related to a theme or topic in the textbook chapter. These exercises call for an orderly presentation of factual material on a topic in the form of notes. Your instructor may prefer to ask broader essay questions; if so, these essay topics, properly answered, will help you prepare for those essays as well as more narrowly focused ones. Whether the essay topic is broad or narrow, the requirement that your arguments be based on fact, not unsupported opinion, is the same.

You cannot always assume that any statement appearing in a history book is backed by extensive research and is indisputable. History is an art, not a science, despite efforts by its practitioners to base their historical judgments on "hard" (quantifiable) data such as census figures or economic statistics. As you work through the skill exercises in this study guide, you can begin to understand the historian's skills and integrate them into your study of history.

Ideally, this book should be used as a basis for class discussion as well as individual study. You should compare your answers with those of other students (preferably in a classroom setting), and with a discussion leader or professor. You should acquire the habit of making decisions and defending them with evidence and arguments against the views of other students. The essay questions in particular will be useful for class discussions, but the other questions, for which the study guide provides answers from the text, should be regarded as points of departure for discussion. Agreement on the facts does not necessarily mean agreement on their meaning; even when the facts are indisputable, there is still plenty of room for disagreement about their significance.

Too often in history classes, the emphasis may seem to be on facts coming from lecture or text, and students may be reluctant to disagree, to argue, to challenge, or to express judgments. This study guide invites you to exercise judgment based upon evidence and reasoned argument, to learn actively, not passively.

The promise and expectation for this book is that, seriously and properly used, it will be a vehicle for thorough review and a key to your improved performance on examinations. It aims to develop thinking skills that will not only result in better overall achievement in history courses, but also establish lasting habits of thought applicable to any situation.

The Research Paper

One of the major functions of historians is to research and write about the past. Nearly all historians consider it a primary responsibility and, perhaps, even the core of a definition of what it really means to be a historian. The thinking skills of the historian used in the process of research and writing are the same thinking skills that are encouraged by the exercises in this book. To "do history" is to do research by employing the historian's critical thinking skills. Therefore, in many history classes the instructor will assign a research paper. Below is a list of guidelines designed to assist you through the process of research to a finished paper. The critical thinking skills developed by the serious use of this study guide should be of great assistance to your research and to the arrangement and writing of the final paper.

Some Suggestions for Research and Writing History:

1. Choose a topic that is manageable, not too broad and general, and yet not so narrow as to require source material not readily available. You may find it helpful to make a reconnaissance trip through your campus library or other research facility to see what, generally, is available. Don't forget the possibility of finding useful material on the Internet. (But remember, should you be tempted simply to download a finished research paper from cyberspace, that your professor, even if he or she is not particularly computer-literate, has only to type a few phrases from your paper into a common search engine in order to find exactly where you got your paper.) *Plagiarism is a serious academic offense and will usually be detected immediately, with grave consequences for you.*

2. Unless the professor has specific instructions on the research paper, orient the topic toward a question, issue, or a comparative study. If you choose only a broad and general topic, your paper is likely to turn out to be a patchwork of descriptions and the rewording of secondary sources without a meaningful thesis or direction. Use primary sources whenever possible and available. Secondary sources are at least one step removed from the actual documents or other evidence; you are at the mercy of another person's judgment whenever you can't go back to the original (primary) sources.

3. Start immediately after the assignment is made acquire books, find articles, read a general review of the issue or data related to the topic. This quick start serves two purposes. First, it allows you to think and plan the research paper at any spare moment. Also, it gives you time to change your mind and switch subjects if the first choice is unworkable. A quick start also means there will be good books on the library shelves; later you are likely to find the books you need have been checked out by someone else.

4. Choose several questions related to the thesis of the paper, as a way to let your paper take more than one direction, depending on the evidence you are able to find.

5. Read and take notes on relevant data. If quotations are involved, quote precisely. Put on the note cards or note book paper the full bibliographical information including the page number. This will avoid confusion when you pull ideas together in final form. Note that your instructor may want to see note cards or other evidence of your work in progress before you hand in the finished paper. (This requirement may be a way of encouraging you not to procrastinate, or it may also be a way to deter you from handing in a research paper you acquired from the Internet or some other source without doing the research that is the heart of a research paper assignment.)

6. Divide your note cards according to subtopics. It is important to know when to stop taking notes and to start writing. Evidence can be collected forever, so a decision must be made as to when enough data is available to write the paper. There is no golden moment for writing. Do not wait. Write when you feel like it and when you don't feel like it. Avoid jargon and slang ("cart before the horse"). Use a variety of sentence structures—complex, compound. Construct paragraphs around a topic and use an introductory sentence. Be concise and try to find the best way to write what you want to say.

7. With a dictionary and thesaurus at hand and your note cards organized, write the paper section by section. Write double or triple space, on one side only. This gives you room to make changes between lines and on the reverse side. Of course, a word processor makes this operation easier.

8. In the introduction, explain what you are doing, the limitations of the paper, and the expected progression of the paper. Comment upon any difficulties in sources and point out the main effort of your work.

9. In a conclusion, summarize what you have proven and what you have not proven (that is, what more remains to be done). Relate, if possible, your conclusion to a broader spectrum—other historical periods or topics or similar issues at other times.

10. The historian's style is normally a statement, followed by evidence and arguments, and then evaluative statements about the relationship between the statement and the evidence. Reading aloud can help you refine style and smoothness. Use the active voice as much as possible.

11. Follow the bibliographical pattern required or suggested by your professor. Find out whether the professor requires footnotes (at the bottom of each page) or endnotes (at the end of the paper). Again, be aware of and be careful to avoid plagiarism (taking another person's ideas or words without giving proper credit).

12. Proofread carefully. Have a friend read the paper also and offer comments or search for mistakes.

13. Save at least one backup file copy, if you are using a computer to write your paper. (If you always assume your computer's hard drive is about to crash, you will make backup copies as you work, and whenever the computer does fail, you will have your data safely stored elsewhere, so you can retrieve your files.)

Brian Gordon

25

Aftermath
The Reconstruction
of the Union, 1865-1877

"I am for negro suffrage in every rebel state. If it be just, it should not be denied, if it be necessary, it should be adopted and if it be a punishment to traitors, they deserve it."

Thaddeus Stevens

"History is little more than the crimes, follies, and misfortunes of mankind."

Edward Gibbon

I. Key Words

You should be able to define the following words and explain their historical significance in relation to the development of American history.

Reconstruction
Abraham Lincoln
Radical Republicans
Lincoln's 10% Plan
freedmen
Wade-Davis Bill
pocket veto
Andrew Johnson
Thaddeus Stevens
Charles Sumner
George W. Julian
Freedmen's Bureau
O. O. Howard
black codes
Fourteenth Amendment
Johnson's "swing around the circle"
Tenure of Office Act
Edwin Stanton
Ulysses S. Grant
Fifteenth Amendment
carpetbaggers
scalawags
"Black" Reconstruction
Ku Klux Klan

Blanche K. Bruce and Hiram Revels
P. B. S. Pinchback
Nathan Bedford Forrest
white supremacy
Jay Gould and Jim Fisk
Crédit Mobilier scheme
"Redeemers"
J. H. Rainey
George H. White
Horace Greeley
Civil Rights Act of 1875
Samuel J. Tilden
Rutherford B. Hayes
Compromise of 1877
"Redeemers"

II. True-False

If the statement is false, change any words necessary to make it true.

1. Reconstruction refers to the political process by which the 11 rebel states were restored to a normal constitutional relationship with the national government.

2. The reconstruction policy Lincoln proposed as early as 1863 was soundly repudiated by his own party.

3. Only Andrew Jackson, of all presidents in the past, had assumed so much authority as Lincoln had during the Civil War.

4. Most of the Radical Republicans were former abolitionists, but they did not usually insist on full civil and political rights for the former slaves.

5. Lincoln vetoed the Wade-Davis Bill and then made a "swing around the circle" speaking tour to explain in detail why he opposed it.

6. Andrew Johnson grew to adulthood illiterate, asked a schoolteacher to teach him how to read, and then married her.

7. Johnson had owned slaves as late as 1862, and did not believe that former slaves should be regarded as citizens.

8. Johnson based his case for presidential supervision on the assumption that the southern states had never left the Union because it was constitutionally impossible to do so.

9. After Johnson pardoned former Confederate leaders, they were eligible to hold office under his reconstruction program. Southern voters then sent many of these rebels to

Congress, but Congress claimed that the southern states had committed suicide by leaving the union, and could therefore be treated as disorganized communities.

10. The reaction of the former slaves to the news of their freedom was to stay on the plantation, since they were not used to having the freedom to travel.

11. Most of the teachers at schools set up by the Freedmen's Bureau were idealistic white women from the North.

12. Although blacks were to be controlled economically under the black codes, the civil liberties listed in the Bill of Rights were accorded them.

13. In the election of 1866, most of the Radical Republicans were tossed out of office.

14. Tennessee was never really affected by Radical Reconstruction.

15. The Radicals attempted to establish the supremacy of the legislature over the judicial and executive branches of the government.

16. Andrew Johnson was impeached in 1868, but the Senate refused to hear the case.

17. Statewide public school systems were not founded in the South prior to Reconstruction.

18. Most of the "scalawags" were, as southern planters described them, "poor white trash."

19. "Black Reconstruction" governments in the South were so named because former slaves, most of them illiterate field hands, dominated the governments of most southern states during Reconstruction.

20. The Crédit Mobilier scheme was a banking scandal during Grant's administration in which Grant, his vice president, and various members of Congress were deeply involved.

III. Multiple Choice

1. When the votes were counted in the 1876 election, the popular vote went to

a. Tilden
b. Hayes
c. Grant
d. Lincoln

2. According to Albion Tourgée, Republicans gave the ballot to men without

a. homes
b. money
c. education
d. any of these

3. Reconstruction in some southern states gave birth to

a. trade
b. paper money
c. public school systems
d. racial integration

4. Most of the articles of impeachment of Andrew Johnson dealt with the

a. drunkenness of Johnson
b. Tenure of Office Act
c. disrespect of Congress
d. Reconstruction policy

5. Among other provisions, the Fourteenth Amendment forbade the Confederate states from

a. setting up sharecropping
b. paying their domestic and foreign debt
c. integrating schools
d. enforcing black codes

6. Blacks who failed to sign labor contracts under the black codes could be arrested and

a. their labor sold to the highest bidder
b. physically punished, whipped
c. deported to the North
d. made to work in a chain gang

7. The rumor was that when Johnson took the presidential oath he was (because of a severe cold)

a. incoherent
b. a dying man
c. unable to read his notes
d. tipsy

8. At the end of the Civil War, southern banks were ruined because they

a. had printed Confederate paper money valued only in hope
b. had their assets confiscated by the Union Army
c. continued to invest in plantations and slaves throughout the war
d. had not seen the end of the war coming

9. The term "Reconstruction" in the context of this chapter refers primarily to

a. the physical rebuilding of war damage in the South, where most of the battles took place
b. reconstruction of the social structure of the nation
c. the political reconstruction of the Union
d. changes in the South's economy in the decades after 1865

10. The Radical position on Lincoln's plan for Reconstruction was

a. Southern states that had tried to secede had in fact never left the Union
b. Readmission of southern states would require a majority of rebels to sign an oath of allegiance to the Union
c. States could "resume their ordinary relationship with the Union" when 10% of 1860 voters took an oath of allegiance
d. always to put the concern for the Union ahead of any other priority

IV. Fill-in Questions

Fill in each blank in the following statements with the correct information.

1. Though much of the South's infrastructure had been destroyed by the Civil War, Reconstruction refers to the process of restoring the _____ rebel states to a normal relationship with the national government.

2. Lincoln declared that as soon as ____ percent of the voters in a Confederate state took an oath of allegiance, the state could be represented in Congress.

3. According to the Wade-Davis Bill, at least _____ percent of the white male citizens of a seceded state had to swear an oath of loyalty before that state could be reconstructed.

4. _____ was the only senator of _____ from the rebel states who remained loyal.

5. By the end of 1865, Johnson had pardoned _____ Confederate leaders.

6. George W. Julian proposed to confiscate planters' land and give freedmen _____-acre farms in order to provide them economic independence.

7. The head of the Freedmen's Bureau was _____.

8. Black codes, which replaced the old slave codes in southern states, defined a _____-class form of citizenship for the freedmen

9. After the 1866 congressional election in which Andrew Johnson campaigned against the _____, they controlled more than _____ of the seats in both houses of Congress, enough to override every _____ that Johnson handed them.

10. The Fortieth Congress in 1867 dissolved the southern state governments and partitioned the Confederacy into _____ military provinces.

11. States met the requirements of Reconstruction at various times. _____ was the first state to be admitted, but four states—_____, _____, _____, and _____ were governed by the military until _____.

12. All but of ____ of the 11 articles of impeachment of Johnson dealt with the Tenure of Office Act.

13. Conviction of an impeached federal official means _____, and requires a _____ vote in the _____.

14. In 1868, the vote in Johnson's case was _____ to _____, meaning he escaped conviction by _____ vote.

15. The results of the 1868 election suggested that the future of the Republican Party seemed to depend on the _____ vote. Consequently, Republicans drafted the _____ Amendment, which said states could not deny the right to vote on the basis of _____. _____, or previous condition of _____.

16. The Republican governor of Louisiana banked $_____ during a year when his salary was $_____.

17. The first post-Reconstruction treasurer of Mississippi absconded with $_____.

18. Blacks were _____ percent of Republican voters in the South, but held only a _____ of public offices.

19. The federal government estimated that the Ku Klux Klan, which was founded by _____, murdered _____ blacks in 1868, and more the next year.

20. _____ of the _____ African Americans in Congress during Reconstruction had been _____.

21. _____ members of Grant's cabinet were involved in corruption.

22. The Civil Rights Act of 1875 was the last significant federal attempt to enforce equal rights for _____ years.

V. Essay Questions

Write notes under each of the following questions that would help you answer similar essay questions on an exam.

1. Compare and contrast the programs and attitudes toward Reconstruction of Abraham Lincoln and Andrew Johnson.

2. Were the Confederate states "conquered provinces" or had they never really separated from the United States? Explain.

3. To what extent were the Radicals morally correct in their goals? What would indicate that they had little interest in the welfare of the blacks?

4. Describe the black codes. Were they a means of transition to real freedom or an act of suppression to overcome the results of the war? Explain.

5. In what ways was Johnson right in his response to the Radical program? How was he wrong?

6. State and explain the meaning of the Fourteenth Amendment.

7. Describe Johnson's campaign in 1866.

8. Explain in detail the Radical Republican program.

9. In what ways did the Radicals attempt to change the system of American government regarding its checks and balances? Would the parliamentary system of government be more effective than the established U.S. system? Why?

10. Describe the impeachment of Andrew Johnson. Was this a political turning point in American history? Why or why not?

11. What is the legend of Reconstruction? What were the realities of governing the postwar South? Should the legend be revised? Why or why not?

12. Describe the election of 1876 in detail. Did the North betray the blacks and the nation by their withdrawal and deal of 1876? Explain.

13. Write a brief essay on the role of blacks in Congress during Reconstruction.

ANSWERS

II. True-False

1. True
2. True
3. False
4. False
5. False
6. True
7. True
8. True
9. True
10. False
11. True
12. False
13. False
14. True
15. True
16. False
17. True
18. False
19. False
20. False

III. Multiple Choice

1. a
2. d
3. c
4. b
5. b
6. a
7. d
8. a
9. c
10. b

IV. Fill-in

1. 11
2. 10%
3. 50%
4. Andrew Johnson; 22
5. 13,000
6. 40
7. O. O. Howard
8. second
9. Radicals; 2/3; veto
10. five
11. Tennessee; Georgia; Mississippi; Texas; Virginia; 1870
12. two
13. removal from office; 2/3; Senate
14. 35; 19; one
15. black; 15th; race; color; servitude
16. $100,000; $8,000
17. $1,777,000
18. 80%; fifth
19. Nathan Bedford Forrest; 700
20. 13; 22; slaves
21. three
22. 80

26

Parties, Patronage, and Pork
Politics in the Late Nineteenth Century

"I am a stalwart! Arthur is president!"

"Vote yourself a pension."

"A historian has to fight against temptations special to his mode of life, temptations from country, class, church, college, party, authority of talents, solicitation of friends."

Lord Acton

I. Key Words

You should be able to define the following words and explain their historical significance in relation to the development of American history.

Samuel Tilden
"Grand Old Party"
"Solid South"
"Yellow Dog Democrats"
swing states
political boss system
Tammany Hall
"Bourbons"
patronage
"pork-barrel" bills
"waving the bloody shirt"
Grand Army of the Republic (GAR)
"Vote yourself a pension"
Rutherford B. Hayes
James A. Garfield
Pendleton Act of 1883
Chester A. Arthur
Grover Cleveland
"rum, romanism, and rebellion"
George Washington Plunkitt
tariff issue
McKinley Tariff of 1890
"greenbacks" and the money issue
deflation and inflation

Greenback Labor Party
"Goo-Goos"
William Marcy ("Boss") Tweed
"sandbagging"
Tammany Hall

II.   True-False

If the statement is false, change any words necessary to make it true.

1. Politics in the late 19th century attracted the most energetic men with "greatness" in them.

2. There was a clear difference in the late 19th century between politics and business.

3. In no other period of American history did a higher percentage of eligible voters actually exercise their right to vote.

4. With the exception of Connecticut, New England voted heavily Democratic.

5. Not a single former slave state voted Republican in a presidential election during the late 19th century.

6. Several presidential elections during the period were decided in New York State where, for the Republicans to win, it was necessary to get a large turnout in New York City.

7. National conventions, which met every four years, played a much more important role in party politics than they do today.

8. In election years the party assessed those with government jobs a modest percentage of their income to finance the campaign.

9. It was possible to grow quite rich legally in government service.

10. Rutherford B. Hayes had a safe desk job throughout the Civil War, even though he was officially a veteran.

11. President Hayes's wife Lucy was ironically called "Lemonade Lucy" because she was an alcoholic.

12. To replace the loss of assessments on office holders for political campaigns, both parties turned to contributions from farmers.

13. Because of a question about his place of birth, Chester A. Arthur may have been president illegally.

14. Grover Cleveland may have fathered an illegitimate child while a lawyer in Buffalo, but he defused the issue by explaining that he was financially supporting the child.

15. Political parties existed in the late 19th century primarily to win power, not to be consistent on issues. All that really mattered was winning elections.

16. Farmers were inclined to favor low tariffs.

17. Deflation means a contraction of the amount of money in circulation; inflation means an increase of the amount of money in circulation.

18. "Machine" politics was notoriously corrupt, but most of the corrupt politicians were quickly exposed and forced to give up their political offices, even if they managed to avoid being sent to prison for their misdeeds. Reform governments replaced corrupt administrations in most cities.

19. Political machines provided substantial income and other rewards for their leaders, but did almost nothing for the ordinary residents of major cities.

20. Most of the big-city political bosses were Irish.

III. Multiple Choice

1. Nationally, the two major political parties

a. merged into one
b. were evenly matched
c. were both weak
d. won each election by a large margin

2. The only presidential candidate of either party between 1872 and 1896 to win a majority of the popular vote was

a. Samuel Tilden
b. Grover Cleveland
c. Rutherford B. Hayes
d. William Jennings Bryan

3. Blacks who retained the right to vote were

a. divided in their party allegiance
b. Democrats
c. Republicans
d. usually for a third party candidate

4. Indiana, Ohio, and New York could determine the outcome of national elections and were called

a. "swing" states
b. vital political entities
c. election states
d. outcome areas

5. The political leaders of the Solid South were named Bourbons because

a. of their extreme conservatism like the French kings
b. they passed around corn liquor
c. they met usually at Bourbon, Louisiana
d. that was a nickname for the Klan

6. Political activists who worked to get the vote out were rewarded with government

a. money
b. assistants
c. employment
d. prestige

7. The Customs Service was remarkably uncorrupt because the collector received

a. official bribes
b. a share of the goods reclaimed from smugglers
c. an extremely high salary
d. severe punishment for cheating

8. The only president elected in the period 1868-1901 who had not been a Union officer during the Civil War was

a. James G. Blaine
b. Benjamin Harrison
c. Grover Cleveland
d. Rutherford B. Hayes

9. From Grant through McKinley, presidents believed that leadership in government should come from

a. the executive
b. the Congress
c. the Supreme Court
d. regulatory agencies within the government

10. The Grand Army of the Republic acted as a political action committee for the

a. Southern veterans of the Civil War
b. Democrats
c. Republicans
d. immigrants and former slaves

11. In 1888, the Republicans ran against Grover Cleveland using the slogan

a. "Vote Yourself a Pension"
b. "Rum, Romanism, and Rebellion"
c. "Semper Fidelis"
d. "His Fraudulency"

12. The second president to be assassinated was

a. Samuel Tilden
b. Rutherford B. Hayes
c. James Garfield
d. Chester A. Arthur

13. The Pendleton Act had what purpose?

a. reform the tariff
b. reform the civil service system
c. regulate railroad rates and service
d. end Reconstruction of the South

14. Small incidents in New York City may have had large results in both the 1884 and 1888 elections. The swing voters in those years may well have been the

a. black voters
b. Irish American voters
c. Civil War veterans
d. recent immigrants

15. George Washington Plunkitt's name for his style of politics-as-business was

a. "honest graft"
b. "dirty business"
c. "stick to the issues"
d. "Hain't I got the power?"

IV. Fill-in Questions

Fill in each blank in the following statements with the correct information.

1. Fully ____ percent of those who were eligible to vote in the 1870s to the 1890s did vote; today, less than _____ of the eligible voters turn out.

2. Two presidential elections were decided by fewer than _____ votes in a total of 9 to 10 million votes.

3. Though the party was actually quite new, the _____ used the nickname "Grand Old Party."

4. Of the 20 presidential and vice presidential slots between 1876 and 1892, men from the swing states filled _____ percent of them, with _____ percent from New York alone.

5. There were _____ government jobs to be given out in Andrew Jackson's time, and _____ by 1871.

6. Government-funded construction projects in a congressman's district for the purpose of rewarding political supporters were called "_____" bills.

7. The River and Harbor Bill of 1886 provided for an expenditure of $_____ million to begin 100 new projects.

8. The Republican practice of reminding voters of the Civil War and the Democratic Party's role in secession was called "waving the _____."

9. As late as 1983, _____ Civil War widows were still receiving a monthly check of about $_____ from the federal government (though the last Union Civil War veteran died more than 30 years earlier.)

10. In the 1880s, the federal government had an unusual financial problem—it was collecting about $_____ million more in taxes than it spent.

11. Though Chester Arthur had been known as the "prince of _____," he signed the first law limiting political parties' use of government jobs for political purposes. That 1883 law was the _____ Act.

12. At first, only _____ percent of 131,000 government workers were protected by civil service. By 1900, _____ percent of the federal government's workers held civil service positions, and about _____ percent of government clerks were women.

13. George Washington Plunkitt's name for his practical style of politics (which today would be called "conflict of interest") was "_____."

14. Most manufacturers favored a _____ tariff.

15. Tariffs moved to a high of _____ percent in the McKinley tariff of 1890.

16. For farmers (as with other debtors), deflation of the economy meant that every dollar borrowed had to be paid back with _____ bushels of wheat or other produce, compared to the amount they anticipated when they went into debt.

17. The New York County Courthouse was a $600,000 building that cost the taxpayers $_____ million to erect.

18. The Tweed Ring looted the city treasury of $ _____ million in only a few years.

19. Boss Tweed dumped $ _____ worth of coal for the poor, and Tim Sullivan gave away _____ turkeys every Christmas.

20. The New York City political machine controlled _____ jobs.

21. Given the choice between reform city governments—many of which tried to cut expenditures by cutting services—and the often-corrupt urban political machines, immigrant voters usually preferred the _____.

V. Essay Questions

Write notes under each of the following questions that would help you answer similar essay questions on an exam.

1. Describe, with appropriate statistics, the system of politics in the late nineteenth century. Was the leadership of Congress and lack of vigorous presidential leadership the way arrangements were supposed to be under our Constitution? Explain.

2. Explain the make-up of the two political parties. How does this compare to the composition of political parties today? Be specific.

3. Evaluate the contribution of James A. Garfield to American politics. Could he have been a great president had he recovered from his wounds? Why or why not?

4. What took place at a party convention? Was this technique better than our present system of selecting candidates? Why or why not?

5. Which was more harmful to politics—patronage, the "bloody shirt," or pork? To what extent does patronage place responsibility on the person in power, since he makes the appointments?

6. Describe the Civil War pension system. Was it really an abuse or did the money go to needy people who had served well? Explain.

7. Which president do you believe had the most ability and performed best as president—Hays, Garfield, Arthur, Cleveland, or Harrison? Give evidence and arguments to support

your choice. What additional evidence would be helpful if you had it available? List this evidence.

8. Explain the Pendleton Act of 1883 and the progress of civil-service reform. Was the move from patronage to big business support for politicians beneficial? Explain.

9. What were some of the smaller incidents that influenced elections of the times? Were Americans more naive then or now? Explain.

10. Describe the tariff issue. Are many parts of the issue still a problem? Explain.

11. Explain the money problem in the late nineteenth century. Why is this issue so irrelevant in contemporary times to the average citizen?

12. Describe the operation of political machines in the cities. Were their social services more humane than the reformers' efforts? Explain.

ANSWERS

II. True-False

1. False
2. False
3. True
4. False
5. True
6. False
7. True
8. True
9. True
10. False
11. False
12. False
13. True
14. True
15. True
16. True
17. True
18. False
19. False
20. True

III. Multiple Choice

1. b
2. a
3. c
4. a
5. a
6. c
7. b
8. c
9. b
10. c
11. a
12. c
13. b
14. b
15. a

IV. Fill-in

1. 80; half
2. 40,000
3. Republicans
4. 90%; 40%
5. 5000; 50,000
6. "pork-barrel"
7. $15
8. "bloody shirt"
9. 41; $70
10. $100
11. spoilsmen; Pendleton
12. 10%; 40%; 30%
13. "honest graft"
14. high
15. 50%
16. more
17. $13
18. $200
19. $50,000; 5,000
20. 20,000
21. machines

27

Big Industry, Big Business Economic Development in the Late Nineteenth Century

"What do I care about the law? Hain't I got the power?"

"The machine in the garden."

" I mean to put a potato in a pillbox."

"The history of the world is the record of man in quest of his daily bread and butter."

H. W. Van Loon

I.   Key Words

You should be able to define the following words and explain their historical significance in relation to the development of American history.

Centennial Exposition of 1876
Corliss steam engine
Mesabi range
Alexander Graham Bell
Thomas A. Edison
Menlo Park
J. P. Morgan
George Westinghouse
direct current and alternating current
standard gauge (for railroads)
standard time zones
Charles F. Dowd
Cornelius Vanderbilt
Daniel Drew
"watered stock"
James Fisk and Jay Gould
"rags to riches"
Cyrus Field
James J. Hill
Pacific Railway Act of 1862
Union Pacific and Central Pacific
railroad land grants

Promontory Point
railroad mania
Panic of 1873
Jay Cooke
steel industry
Henry Bessemer
Andrew Carnegie
vertical integration
U.S. Steel
limited liability corporation
John D. Rockefeller
"black gold"
Kerosene
Edwin Drake
horizontal integration
Standard Oil Company
rebates and drawbacks
trusts and monopolies

II. True-False

If the statement is false, change any words necessary to make it true.

1. In the Centennial Exposition of 1876, the emphasis was on political heritage and the Declaration of Independence.

2. The Corliss steam engine at the Centennial Exposition in Philadelphia in 1876 was the largest steam engine ever built.

3. By 1860, the United States was already the largest industrial nation in the world.

4. Because of the importance of industry, factory workers were a significant force in American politics during the late 19th century.

5. American industrial growth was helped both by European investors and by immigration from Europe.

6. American iron ore was richer and more plentiful than any other country's.

7. Though Bell got the credit, the telephone was actually invented by Thomas Edison.

8. The most important of Edison's inventions was the air brake.

9. By 1865, the United States was already the world's premier railway country, with about 35,000 miles of track.

10. The standard American railroad gauge (the distance between the rails) was derived from English practice, which in turn was based on the width of Roman wagon wheel ruts.

11. The idea of standard time and time zones was enacted into law at the behest of the nation's railroads.

12. Commodore Vanderbilt was quick to point out the responsibilities of the businessman to consider social and ethical factors in his business dealings.

13. Though "rags to riches" was a common catchphrase, Andrew Carnegie was the only major industrialist who started life in poverty.

14. The largest ship in the world, the *Great Eastern*, failed as a passenger carrier but laid the first successful transatlantic telegraph cable.

15. The Erie Railroad, though managed by scoundrels, was actually one of the nation's safest and most innovative railroads.

16. Of all the transcontinental railroads, only the Great Northern was built without public funding.

17. In 1862 Congress committed the American people to underwriting the construction of a transcontinental railroad by giving away land.

18. Indians helped build the transcontinental railroads and seemed not to sense that these railroads meant an end to their way of life.

19. The Atchison, Topeka, and Santa Fe railroad at first did not enter Santa Fe, but built its station at Albuquerque.

20. Andrew Carnegie applied the principle of vertical integration to reduce his costs and thus increase his advantage over his competitors in the steel business.

21. Controlling an industry by controlling a key portion of its process is known as horizontal integration.

22. John D. Rockefeller explained that the goal of the Standard Oil Trust was to make as much money as possible, by whatever means he could get away with.

23. With each step toward monopoly, Standard Oil reduced the price of kerosene.

24. Despite Rockefeller's best efforts, Standard Oil never controlled more than 3 or 4 percent of the American oil business.

25. Andrew Carnegie bragged that he could produce a pound of steel for a penny.

III. Multiple Choice

1. When President Ulysses S. Grant visited the Centennial Exposition to open the fair, he did so at the

   a. case containing the Declaration of Independence
   b. Philadelphia mayor's office
   c. site of the giant Corliss steam engine
   d. Carpenter's Hall

2. Which of the following was not a characteristic of the Vanderbilt railroad line?

   a. standard gauge tracks
   b. steel rails
   c. use of air brakes
   d. frequent and bloody wrecks

3. Thomas Edison's most important invention was the

   a. phonograph
   b. telegraph
   c. incandescent light bulb
   d. photography

4. Which of the following was not a problem of building the transcontinental railroad?

   a. snows in the Sierra Nevada
   b. finding hard-working laborers
   c. Indians
   d. narrow and steep passes in the mountains

5. To Thomas A. Edison, invention was just another kind of

   a. hard work
   b. inspiration and insight
   c. luck
   d. creative act

6. John D. Rockefeller sought to control the "narrows" in oil, that is, the

   a. oil fields
   b. transportation to refineries
   c. by-products of refining
   d. refining process

7. According to the text, the invention that conquered American geography was the

a. telegraph
b. telephone
c. steam railroad
d. national highway system

8. Andrew Carnegie made his largest fortune by investing in

a. telegraphy
b. railroads
c. steelmaking
d. Edison's companies

9. The first billion dollar corporation was

a. United States Steel
b. Standard Oil Corporation
c. Pennsylvania Railroad
d. Union Pacific/Central Pacific Railroad

10. Alternating current, which made possible long distance transmission of electricity, was the contribution of

a. J. P. Morgan
b. Alexander Graham Bell
c. Thomas Edison
d. George Westinghouse

IV. Fill-in Questions

Fill in each blank in the following statements with the correct information.

1. Between 1865 and 1900 the population of the United States changed from ____ million to ____ million.

2. At the end of the Civil War, the annual production of goods in the U.S. was valued at $____ billion; by 1900 it was $____ billion.

3. In 1860, the United States was the _____ largest industrial nation in the world, with more than _____ factories.

4. By 1914, fully ____ percent of the world's industrial and mining economy was American, more than the combined shares of _____ and _____.

5. Foreign investors poured more than $_____ billion into American industrial growth, allowing Americans to divert less than _____ percent of their national income to support such growth, far less than the percentage most countries before or since had to invest.

6. The "Wizard of Menlo Park" was _____. He took out more than _____ patents between 1876 and 1900.

7. George Westinghouse's _____ made railroads safer and trains longer. Later he challenged Edison's dominance of the electrical power industry by perfecting the means to transmit _____ current.

8. In 1865, in the former Confederacy, there were _____ railroad companies with an average track length of only _____ miles each.

9. Before the Civil War a cargo going by rail from Chicago to New York had to be unloaded and reloaded _____ times.

10. Before the advent of standard time, there were _____ time zones in the United States; after 1883 there were just _____.

11. Standard gauge for American railroads is _____ feet, _____ inches.

12. In the final days of construction, work crews for the Central Pacific Railroad laid _____ miles of track in just one day.

13. Most of the laborers on the Central Pacific were _____; the typical Union Pacific worker was _____.

14. The federal government gave the land-grant railroads a total of _____ million acres and state governments added _____ million acres.

15. In 1872, only _____ railroad in _____ made a profit.

16. The government lent the two companies that built the transcontinental railroad between $_____ and $_____ per mile of track (at low interest rates) and granted them one half of the land in a _____ mile-wide area where they laid track.

17. His personal income climbed to $ _____ million per year and Carnegie sold out in 1901 for $ _____ million.

18. Corporations, according to court interpretations of the Fourteenth Amendment, had the same rights as _____

19. "Black Gold" was another name for _____.

20. Within 20 years of its founding, Standard Oil controlled _____ percent of the refining business.

V. Essay Questions

Write notes under each of the following questions that would help you answer similar essay questions on an exam.

1. What were the benefits and harm done by the rapid expansion of the railroad network?

2. To what extent should railroad entrepreneurs (Vanderbilt, Thompson, Stanford) be praised and to what extent condemned for their behavior as businessmen?

3. List and explain briefly the causes of rapid American industrial growth in the last half of the nineteenth century.

4. To what extent can the rapid industrial growth of the United States in the late nineteenth century serve as a model for underdeveloped nations today?

5. Should the federal government and the courts have come down hard on railroads in order to avoid many of the injustices that emerged from their rapid growth?

6. In what ways did governments (town, state, and national) aid the building of railroads? Was it a proper use of the power and resources of government to give this aid? Explain.

7. Describe the invention and the impact on society of the telephone. What were its benefits and what might be considered its harmful effects? Explain.

8. Describe the accomplishments of the Field Brothers. In what specific ways might they be considered an example of the American ideal of social mobility?

9. React to Vanderbilt's belief that ethics and social responsibility had no place in the counting room, and since he had the power he wasn't concerned about the law. Give examples of how this attitude expressed itself in action. Is the fact that he did build and consolidate railroads a partial justification for such an attitude? Explain.

10. Were telephone and the typewriter liberating for women? Why or why not?

11. What were the keys to Thomas Edison's success? List his inventions and then rank them according to their impact on society. Explain your ranking. Is Edison an ideal American in his attitude and way of life? Why or why not?

12. Describe the development of Andrew Carnegie's steel empire. To what extent was he a genius and to what extent lucky? Explain.

13. Describe the rise of John D. Rockefeller in the business world. Would you consider him an industrial giant and genius or a ruthless capitalist without concern for ethics? Explain.

ANSWERS

II. True-False

1. False
2. True
3. False
4. False
5. True
6. True
7. False
8. False
9. True
10. True
11. True
12. False
13. True
14. True
15. False
16. True
17. True
18. False
19. True
20. True
21. True
22. False
23. True
24. False
25. True

III. Multiple Choice

1. c
2. d
3. c
4. b
5. a
6. d
7. c
8. c
9. a
10. d

IV. Fill-in

1. 36; 76
2. $2; $13
3. fourth; 100,000
4. 46; Germany; Great Britain
5. $3.4; 14%
6. Thomas A. Edison; 1,000
7. air brake; alternating
8. 400; 40
9. six
10. 80; four
11. 4; 8 ½
12. 10.6
13. Chinese; Irish
14. 131; 45
15. one; three
16. $16,000; $48,000; 40
17. $25; $500
18. persons
19. crude oil
20. 90%

28

Living with Leviathan
Reactions to Big Business and Great Wealth

"unrestricted competition"
"antisocial and anti-Christian"
"tainted money"
"To know the truth of history is to realize its ultimate myth and its inevitable ambiguity."

Roy B. Baster

I. Key Words

You should be able to define the following words and explain their historical significance in relation to the development of American history.

California's "Big Four"
Collis P. Huntington
Leland Stanford
Mark Hopkins
Charles Crocker
Southern Pacific Railroad
The Octopus
Patrons of Husbandry (Grange)
Granger laws
Munn v. Illinois (1877)
Wabash case (*Wabash, St. Louis, and Pacific Railway Co. v. Illinois*)
Interstate Commerce Act (1887)
Interstate Commerce Commission
"money power"
J. P. Morgan
James B. Duke
Sherman Antitrust Act of 1890
U.S. v. E.C. Knight Company (1895)
Henry George
"single tax"
Edward Bellamy
Looking Backward: 2000-1887
Marxists
Haymarket bombing
Social Gospel
Walter Rauschenbusch and Washington Gladden
Social Darwinism

Herbert Spencer
William Graham Sumner
Gospel of Success
Russell Conwell
Horatio Alger
philanthropy
Andrew Carnegie
Thorstein Veblen
"conspicuous consumption"
Newport "cottages"
Tin Pan Alley
Frank Leslie's Illustrated Newspaper

II.   True-False

If the statement is false, change any words necessary to make it true.

1. Railroads were the first big business.

2. In 1877 in *Munn v. Illinois* the Supreme Court decided that the public interest could not interfere with the operation of a private business.

3. The ICC had no real power.

4. Every railroad but one—the Great Northern—prospered throughout the 1890s.

5. After the "money power" took over many railroads, wasteful competition declined, but so did shipping rates.

6. J.P. Morgan was the richest of all the Jewish bankers who were sometimes blamed for the nation's financial problems during hard times.

7. In contrast to the weak Interstate Commerce Act, the Sherman Antitrust Act was a powerful tool to control the power of business combinations.

8. Henry George's "single tax" was his proposal to abolish all taxes except for a high tariff on imported goods.

9. Edward Bellamy's novel *Looking Backward* imagined a world in which socialism replaced capitalism, and was maintained in power by a tyrannical central government that controlled wealth for the benefit of powerful bureaucrats.

10. The tragic irony of the Haymarket bombing in 1886 was that police officers, who had been on the side of strikers prior to the bombing, were the majority of the victims killed.

11. According to the Social Gospel, churches ought to work for the relief of the poor and a more equitable distribution of wealth.

12. Social Darwinism was the law of the jungle applied to human society.

13. According to the "gospel of success," the existence of poverty was due to problems with the economic system itself, and if it could be reformed, everyone would be rich.

14. In a typical story by Horatio Alger, the young hero goes from rags to riches simply by his own hard work.

15. None of the richest American businessmen did much to help racial minorities or poor people get ahead.

16. Many millionaires bought yachts just so they could say that they owned one.

17. Women's fashions were designed to emphasize the activity and movement of the wealthy.

18. Ordinary Americans knew of the shenanigans of the very rich through direct observation and servants' stories.

19. Tin Pan Alley, center of the sheet-music industry, preached the traditional view that the rich were virtuous and received their riches as their just reward.

20. By the end of the century, many large daily papers bumped conventional news to the back pages when an upper-class scandal came up in the courts.

III. Multiple Choice

1. The idea that seemed to mock the American value of hard work was that one could

a. be lazy and get by
b. grow richer while not working
c. be fired after working hard
d. live off the land

2. Many of the wealthy lived to spend money, what Thorstein Veblen called

a. conspicuous consumption
b. putting it back in the system
c. paying their debts
d. obnoxious

3. A fad among the very rich that aggravated many Americans was the rush during the 1880s and 1890s

a. to build homes at Palm Beach
b. to buy yachts
c. to marry their daughters to European nobles
d. to have plenty of servants

4. The chief consumers in the wealthy families were the

a. women
b. young children
c. in-laws
d. guests

5. One group that was intimately familiar with the kind of wealth the rich enjoyed was the

a. wealthy of Europe
b. teachers and professors
c. factory workers
d. tradesmen and repairmen

6. After Jim Fisk was shot by a rival for the affections of a showgirl, the newspapers dwelled on

a. the morality of the rich
b. the sumptuous personal life of Fisk
c. the immorality of the theater
d. the rising crime rate

7. Because the revenue from taxing the "unearned increment" would be so high, Henry George called it a

a. single tax
b. bonanza
c. technique to avoid class rebellion
d. revolutionary tax

8. Those who organized the rally in support of strikers at Haymarket Square were

a. businessmen
b. Marxists
c. union organizers
d. anarchists

9. In the Wabash case of 1886, the Supreme Court ruled that

a. states can regulate interstate railroad rates if a railroad comes into that state
b. states can regulate interstate railroads, but only within that state
c. only the Congress can regulate interstate railroads
d. neither federal nor state governments can regulate interstate railroads

10. The slogan often used by Social Darwinists was

a. "survival of the fittest"
b. "from each according to his ability; to each according to his needs"
c. "business leaders should be chosen by election, not selection"
d. "poverty is a sin"

IV. Fill-in Questions

Fill in each blank in the following statements with the correct information.

1. The second biggest landowner in California was the _____.

2. Frank Norris's novel of 1901, _____, depicted the railroad's tentacles reaching into every corner of the state of California.

3. In 1869, there were _____ local chapters of the Patrons of Husbandry; by the mid-1870s, there were _____, with _____ dues-paying members.

4. By the early 1890s, the major railroad trunk lines were consolidated into _____ great systems.

5. Between 1866 and 1897, the cost of shipping a hundred pounds of grain from Chicago to New York dropped from _____ cents to _____ cents.

6. The sugar trust controlled about _____ percent of the business.

7. During the first ten years of the Sherman Act, only _____ cases were instituted and _____ of these were aimed at labor unions.

8. Between 1890 and 1901, the amount of money invested in trusts rose to $_____ million, up from $_____ million.

9. Edward Bellamy's version of a non-Marxian socialism was called _____.

10. Though no evidence linked any particular anarchist to the Haymarket bombing, _____ were brought to trial, and _____ were hanged.

11. According to Herbert Spencer, the ultimate result of shielding men from the effects of folly is to fill the world with _____.

12. Social Darwinism described the growth of big business as "survival of the _____."

13. Russell B. Conwell delivered his pro-wealth lecture, "Acres of Diamonds," more than _____ times.

14. Horatio Alger's books on success for the younger generation sold ____ million copies between 1867 and 1899. He wrote _____ books on the same theme.

15. Thorstein Veblen's name for wasteful and impractical spending by the idle rich was _____.

16. ____ million women worked in domestic service at the end of the century.

17. California's "Big Four" controlled the _____.

18. Some high society parties lasted but a few hours but cost more than $_____.

19. The "machine in the garden" was the _____.

20. J. P. Morgan owned three successively larger yachts called _____.

V. Essay Questions

Write notes under each of the following questions that would help you answer similar essay questions on an exam.

1. Describe the life of the very rich at the end of the nineteenth century. Was this conspicuous consumption beneficial in that it gave work to many people who produced the material goods? Explain.

2. What was the place of women in this society? How would a women's liberation advocate react to this? Explain.

3. Explain why the existence of the idle rich convicted with American ideals.

4. What were Henry George's arguments as a cure to the inequality of wealth?

5. Summarize Edward Bellamy's ideas. Was his economic theory reasonable? Explain.
6. Explain the Social Gospel. Why was this interpretation of Christianity controversial?

7. Which of the critics of the new order seemed to have the most realistic answers to the inequality of wealth—George, Bellamy, or Lloyd? Give reasons for your answers.

8. Describe the "gospel of success" and its expression in Horatio Alger's writing. Were these books accurate guides to the way society worked? Why or why not?

9. Explain the ideas and arguments of Social Darwinism. What was Lester Frank Ward's view of Social Darwinism?

10. Comment on Bradley Martin's idea of having a costume ball to help end the depression. What results came from this ball?

11. What were the varieties of Marxist beliefs in America? How much of a chance did Marxism have in the American economic and political system?

12. Describe the efforts to regulate railroads and big business. Why was regulation usually ineffective?

13. What did the Patrons of Husbandry try to accomplish? How effective were the reforms they made?

14. Which served the nation's economic development best—competition or consolidation? Use examples from major industries to support your argument.

15. What does the text mean by the phrase "women as decor"?

16. Explain the difference between Social Darwinism and Lester Frank Ward's concept of Reform Darwinism.

ANSWERS

II. True-False

1. True
2. False
3. True
4. False
5. True
6. False
7. False
8. False
9. False
10. False
11. True
12. True
13. False
14. False
15. False
16. True
17. False
18. False
19. False
20. True

III. Multiple Choice

1. b
2. a
3. c
4. a
5. d
6. b
7. a
8. d
9. c
10. a

IV. Fill-in

1. Southern Pacific Railroad
2. *The Octopus*
3. 39; 20,000; 800,000
4. five
5. 65; 20
6. 95%
7. 18; 4
8. $326; $192
9. Nationalism
10. eight; four
11. fools
12. fittest
13. 6,000
14. 20; 130
15. conspicuous consumption
16. two
17. Southern Pacific Railroad
18. $100,000
19. railroad
20. *Corsair*

29

We Who Built America
Factories and Immigrants

"Don't get too great a percentage of all one nationality . . . mix them up and obliterate clannishness and selfish social prejudices."

"History is not an arena of justice, it is a test of the capacity to act."
George VIII

I. Key Words

You should be able to define the following words and explain their historical significance in relation to the development of American history.

"aristocracy of labor"
child labor
cultural lag
women's labor
Homestead strike
George Pullman
American Railway Union
Molly Maguires
William Sylvis
National Labor Union
Noble and Holy Order of the Knights of Labor
Uriah Stephens
"yellow-dog contracts"
Terence Powderly
James Cardinal Gibbons
Labor Day
Samuel Gompers
American Federation of Labor
"bread and butter" union goals
emigration and immigration
"new" immigration, compared to "old" immigration
steerage class aboard ships
Ellis Island
"birds of passage"
American Protective Association
"NINA"
Chinese immigration
Chinese Exclusion Act of 1882
Carl Schurz

214

Sephardic and German Jews
Reform Judaism

II. True-False

If the statement is false, change any words necessary to make it true.

1. Between 1860 and 1900 the size of the American working class doubled.

2. As wages fell in the late 19th century, the American standard of living also fell.

3. The skilled "aristocracy of labor" experienced a decline in purchasing power and earnings from 1860 to 1900.

4. The steel industry operated seven days a week, with workers on 12-hour shifts.

5. Though workers' pay was low, at least most businesses took responsibility for workers' safety on the job.

6. One reason for child labor was the fact that children had always worked on farms and in small shops; factory work did not seem all that different.

7. In 1900, about half the workers in textile mills were women.

8. By 1900, more than half the nation's black population had left the South for industrial work in the North and East.

9. Absenteeism plagued the factories of the late nineteenth century, especially during good times.

10. Women in the late nineteenth century were paid the same wages as men in the textile industry.

11. The Molly Maguires was a secret society of Cornish, Welsh, and American miners who tried to improve conditions in the coal mines by threatening terror against the mine owners.

12. Both the National Labor Union and the Knights of Labor tried to improve working conditions by using political action, rather than solidarity in the workplace.

13. Like the American Federation of Labor, the Knights of Labor excluded women, blacks, and immigrants, particularly Roman Catholics.

14. The goal of the American Federation of Labor, according to Samuel Gompers, was to promote long-term utopian reform, including socialism.

15. In each of the six years after 1900, more than a million immigrants arrived in the United States.

16. By 1907, nearly all of the immigrants coming to the U.S. were from southern and eastern Europe.

17. A western lumber magnate explained that in order to have a tractable workforce, an employer should hire from only one ethnic group.

18. American industrialists opposed immigration and called for laws to limit it.

19. "Birds of passage" were immigrants who came to the U.S. to work only for a short time before returning to their homeland.

20. In 1882 Congress enacted the Exclusion Act, which forbade Japanese, Chinese, and Filipino immigration.

21. German Jews clung to their religious heritage but otherwise quickly adopted American mores and customs.

22. Few immigrants had more trouble adapting to American culture than did the Norwegians and Swedes.

III. Multiple Choice

1. In almost every manufacturing area, steam-powered machines took over from artisans and "mechanics," and in their places came

   a. automation
   b. machine tenders
   c. skilled workers
   d. managers

2. Since 1840 the working day for most government employees was

   a. sunrise to sunset
   b. a twelve-hour day
   c. dependent upon the administration
   d. an eight-hour day

3. If a worker was hurt because his machine was dangerous, the employer

   a. was not liable
   b. was liable only for direct medical costs
   c. was liable but often got out of it
   d. paid a flat fee settled ahead of time

4. At the end of the nineteenth century, the skilled workers were overwhelmingly

a. of eastern European background
b. from recent immigrants
c. of old American or British stock
d. migrating farm workers

5. The founders of the first American textile mills had not been able to imagine factory work as a suitable lifetime career for the head of a family, so the first industrial workers were

a. women
b. children
c. blacks
d. unmarried men

6. When the pace became too taxing, the industrial worker would often resort to

a. strikes
b. religion
c. looking for another job
d. sabotage of the machinery

7. The Irish, Scots, Welsh, English, Scandinavians, and Germans were called the

a. Germanic influence
b. "Old Immigration"
c. nation's backbone
d. "New Immigration"

8. Jews in Russia were forbidden to

a. own land
b. buy and sell goods
c. worship God
d. emigrate to America

9. Cornish immigrants helped the American economy by bringing the skills of

a. textile work
b. labor organization
c. politics
d. mining

10. Who belonged to the "aristocracy of labor"?

a. factory workers of any kind, compared to farm laborers
b. highly trained craftsmen and skilled workers
c. the most recent immigrants from Europe by about 1900
d. all workers employed (in any capacity) by the largest corporations, such as Carnegie Steel

IV. Fill-in Questions

Fill in each blank in the following statements with the correct information.

1. In 1860, ____ million Americans made their living in workshops and mills. By 1900, ____ million did.

2. In 1870 the average workshop employed ____ people; however, by 1900 the average worker was one of ____ employees and in some cases had hundreds of co-workers.

3. Taken as a whole, the industrial working class enjoyed almost ____ percent more purchasing power in 1900 than in 1860.

4. The average work week was ____ hours in 1860, and ____ hours in 1910.

5. In the steel industry workers were divided into two shifts of 12 hours each and worked ____ days a week.

6. Between 1880 and 1900, ____ American workers were killed on the job, an average of about one every ____ days.

7. In 1900 the socialist writer John Spargo estimated that ____ million children under 16 years of age were employed full time.

8. In 1900 almost ____ percent of the total workforce was female and half the workers in textiles were women.

9. In 1900, ____ million women were employed for subsistence wages or less in domestic service.

10. More than ____ percent of the black population in 1900 lived in the South, most of them on the land.

11. In one year between 1885 and 1886, the Knights of Labor grew from _____ members to _____.

12. The American Federation of Labor was founded by _____.

13. After the turn of the century, during each of six years, more than ____ million people arrived to make homes in the United States. Most were processed through New York's famous _____.

14. Before 1880 only _____ people of southern and eastern Europe lived in the United States, but between 1880 and 1910 about ____ million arrived.

15. Competition among steamship companies reduced the cheapest transatlantic fare in steerage class to below $_____ by the 1890s.

16. About ____ million Irish came to the United States between 1845 and 1900.

17. The American Protective Association (APA) tried to protect the nation against _____.

18. In 1877 the Chinese represented ____ percent of California's population.

19. By 1900 there were about _____ German-language newspapers being published in the United States.

20. German Jews, led by Rabbi Isaac Mayer Wise, founded _____ Judaism.

V. Essay Questions

Write notes under each of the following questions that would help you answer similar essay questions on an exam.

1. Describe the impact of technology on the working man, in his capacity as a consumer as well as a producer.

2. Explain the important statistical data that describe the workers' problems regarding wages, hours, and conditions of labor.

3. Describe the labor force in the late nineteenth century. Was the use of women and children as workers exploitive or necessary for family income? Explain.

4. Compare and contrast the early labor organizations (Molly Maguires, National Labor Union, and the Knights of Labor) to the AFL. Which was more effective? Why?

5. Did Samuel Gompers betray the labor movement by excluding the unskilled, women, and blacks? Why or why not?

6. Why was Gompers successful in his labor organization? Should he be considered a labor hero? Why or why not?

7. What jobs were blacks usually allowed to do? Where was this population concentrated in 1900?

8. What were the differences between the old immigration and the new immigration?

9. What was meant by the phrase "birds of passage" in relation to American immigration?

10. Describe the adaptation of Germans, Scandinavians, and Jews to America.

ANSWERS

II. True-False

1. False
2. False
3. False
4. True
5. False
6. True
7. True
8. False
9. True
10. False
11. False
12. False
13. False
14. False
15. True
16. True
17. False
18. False
19. True
20. False
21. True
22. False

III Multiple Choice

1. b
2. d
3. a
4. c
5. a
6. d
7. b
8. a
9. d
10. b

IV. Fill-in

1. 1.5; 6
2. 8; 25
3. 50
4. 66; 55
5. 7
6. 35,000; 2
7. 1.8
8. 20
9. 2
10. 80
11. 110,000; 700,000
12. Samuel Gompers
13. 1; Ellis Island
14. 200,000; 8.4
15. $20
16. 3.4
17. Irish Catholic immigrants
18. 17%
19. 800
20. Reform

30

Bright Lights and Slums
The Growth of Big Cities

"Form follows function"

Louis Sullivan

"He who acts as well as watches acquires kinds of knowledge unavailable to him who watches only."

Staughton Lynd

I.   Key Words

You should be able to define each of the following words and explain their historical significance in relation to the development of American history.

assimilation
immigrant aid institutions
settlement houses
Hull House
Jane Addams
Lillian Wald
Henry Street Settlement
the "walking" city
elevated railways and electric trolleys
Elisa Graves Otis
Louis Sullivan and Frank Lloyd Wright
"form follows function"
John and Washington Roebling
Brooklyn Bridge
sweatshops
piecework system
tenements
Jacob Riis
How the Other Half Lives
"dumbbell" tenements
"street Arabs"

II. True-False

If the statement is false, change any words necessary to make it true.

1. Greeks, Armenians, and Italians, though Caucasians, often found themselves on the dark side of America's "color line."

2. Americans who visited immigrant neighborhoods were unsettled because even the smells in the air seemed alien.

3. Settlement houses were established to provide housing for the urban poor.

4. Despite its rural history, the U.S. by 1900 was one of the world's most urbanized nations.

5. New immigrants usually came to the cities, but few native-born rural Americans were interested in leaving their farms and small towns.

6. "Walking" cities were characterized by a clear division among residential, commercial, and manufacturing neighborhoods, with homeless people living at the heart of the city.

7. Electric trolleys were as important to the urbanization of the United States as the railroads were to the settlement of the West.

8. The Brooklyn Bridge ignited a building boom that made Brooklyn the fourth largest city in the United States.

9. The Brooklyn Bridge was the largest and finest example of a stone and cast-iron bridge.

10. The urban death rate was significantly lower than the national average for the time, especially for children.

11. In 1890s, parts of New York City were twice as congested as Charles Dickens's London.

12. The name "dumbbell" tenement was a snide comment about the mental capacity of people who lived in that type of building.

13. Once established, city people were unlikely to move to the country.

14. By 1900 the Roman Catholic faith was the nation's largest single denomination.

15. Old-stock Americans created the settlement house to help immigrants assimilate into American society.

III. Multiple Choice

1. For the most part immigrants clustered together with their own ethnic group in

   a. southern sections of cities
   b. ghettos
   c. mixed streets of ethnic families
   d. areas near rivers

2. Old-stock immigrants to the United States had come primarily from

   a. northern and western Europe
   b. northern and eastern Europe
   c. southern and western Europe
   d. central and eastern Europe

3. Many immigrants joined the American quest for material success by pursuing careers in

   a. banking
   b. education
   c. respectable professions
   d. areas considered not quite respectable

4. Sephardic and German Jewish families who were comfortably established in the United States

   a. ignored the plight of later arrivals
   b. invited newly arrived Jews into their homes
   c. founded a society to aid Eastern European Jews
   d. converted to Christianity

5. Old-stock Americans, in an effort to assist immigrants in coming to terms with America,

   a. created settlement houses
   b. found jobs for them
   c. tried to make them Christians and Protestants
   d. made them feel welcome, regardless of their habits and traditions

6. Americas had an engrained prejudice against cities that dated back to

   a. the Great Awakening
   b. Abraham Lincoln
   c. Thomas Jefferson
   d. the Puritans

7. The total number of farm families grew during the late nineteenth century; while the proportion of farmers in the total population

a. increased
b. declined
c. remained the same
d. nearly doubled

8. The "other half" described in Jacob Riis's book *How the Other Half Lives* were

a. Europeans who did not emigrate to America
b. America's forgotten rural people, particularly in the South
c. recent immigrants living in urban ghettos
d. blacks, Hispanics and other minorities

9. In a typical neighborhood in a "walking" city, a visitor could find all but which of these:

a. small businesses
b. diverse social classes
c. small lots, whether the owner of the property was rich or poor
d. parks and trees

10. William Jenney's contribution to urban growth was the

a. safety elevator
b. suspension bridge
c. I-beam steel girder
d. electric trolley

IV. Fill-in

Fill in the blank(s) in each of the following statements with the correct information.

1. The fate of most immigrants was _____ work at _____ jobs.

2. The Roman Catholic population grew from _____ million in 1880 to _____ million in 1900.

3. In 1790, only _____ percent of Americans lived in towns of 8,000 people or more. By 1900, the portion was _____ percent.

4. In 1790 there were only _____ American cities having a population of 8,000 or more; by 1910, there were _____.

5. In 1890, only _____ percent of the _____ million blacks in the United States lived in cities.

6. Chicago increased its size _____ times in a generation, from 100,000 to _____ million by 1900.

7. The key to growth, for both metropolises and smaller cities, was the _____, pioneered by Frank J. Sprague.

8. Elisha Graves Otis contributed to urban growth by perfecting the _____.

9. _____ million people crossed the Brooklyn Bridge each year. At least _____ workers were killed building it.

10. In contrast to the earlier custom of having clothes tailor-made, by 1900, _____ Americans in _____ were wearing ready-made ("off the rack") clothes.

11. In one Chicago slum as late as 1900, the infant mortality rate was _____ per 1000. The figure for today is less than _____ per 1000.

12. Jacob Riis found that _____ people lived in a square mile of New York slums, equivalent to almost _____ people per acre.

13. The pollution problem associated with urban transportation in the 19th century was _____.

14. There were _____ homeless people in New York City in 1890.

15. The rate of homicide and other serious crimes _____ in American cities during the 1880s.

V. Essay Questions

Write notes under each of the following questions that would help you answer similar questions on an exam.

1. What did "assimilation" mean for new immigrants? What forces encouraged and discouraged assimilation?

2. Describe the new immigrants, especially compared to the old-stock immigrants.

3. What were the features of an immigrant ghetto?

4. How could immigrants get ahead in America? Why could limit their opportunity in the land of opportunity?

5. What institutions helped immigrants adjust to life in America?

6. Explain the function of settlement houses. What was the significant difference between settlement houses and tenements?

7. Explain the reasons for the movement of young rural people to the city. What was so attractive about cities, especially for young people?

8. Describe the evolution of transportation systems in American cities.

9. What were the problems in "building up," that is, building multi-storied buildings? How were these problems solved?

10. Describe the building of and the impact of the Brooklyn Bridge. Was it beneficial for Brooklyn? Why or why not?

11. Write an essay on the problems of living in the city in the 1890s. Which of the problems were most serious? Compare city living a century ago with the problems and advantages of city living today.

12. Describe the sweatshop system. Why could it exist, and what opportunities did it provide for the owners and workers? Who benefited most from the system?

ANSWERS

II. True-False

1. True
2. True
3. False
4. True
5. False
6. False
7. True
8. True
9. False
10. False
11. True
12. False
13. True
14. True
15. True

III. Multiple Choice

1. b
2. a
3. d
4. c
5. a
6. c
7. b
8. c
9. d
10. c

IV. Fill-in Questions

1. hard; menial
2. 6; 10
3. 3.4%; 33%
4. 6; 778
5. 12%; 5
6. 20; 2.2
7. electric trolley car
8. elevator (safety hoist)
9. 33; 20
10. 9; 10
11. 200; 20
12. 330,000; 1,000
13. horse manure
14. 14,000
15. tripled

31

The Last Frontier
Winning the Last of the West, 1865 -1900

"To whom does this land belong? I believe, it belongs to me ... I hope you will listen to me."

Bear Rib, Sioux

"This I regard as history's highest function, to let no worthy action be uncommemorated, and to hold out the reprobation of posterity as a terror to evil words and deeds."

Tacitus

I. Key Words

You should be able to define each of the following words and explain their historical significance in relation to the development of American history.

Frontier (in both the European and American uses of the term)
Pony Express
Rocky Mountains
the Great Basin
Great Plains
Navajo
Indian Territory
"civilized tribes"
Plains Indians
nomadic tribes
bison (buffalo)
George Crook
"buffalo soldiers"
George Armstrong Custer
Battle of the Little Bighorn ("Custer's Last Stand")
A Century of Dishonor
Richard Henry Pratt
Carlisle Indian School
Dawes Severalty Act of 1887
Jack Wilson (Wovoka)
Ghost Dance
Wounded Knee
cattle kingdom

vaqueros
"cowtowns"
Abilene
Joseph G. McCoy
Texas longhorns
rail head
blizzard of 1886
Ned Buntline
pulp novels
"Wild Bill" Hickok
Calamity Jane
"Buffalo Bill" Cody
mining frontier
gold and silver rushes
Comstock Lode

II. True-False

If the statement is false, change any words necessary to make it true.

1. Half of the state of Texas was not settled until after the Civil War.

2. Where trees did not grow, Americans believed that agriculture was impossible.

3. The Pony Express system was abandoned after only 18 months, mostly because only a few riders managed to get across the desert West without being killed by Indians or having their horses die of thirst.

4. The Navajo were skilled weavers of cotton; the introduction of Spanish sheep gave them the raw material to weave wool as well.

5. The tribes of the Great Plains were a source of awe and admiration to easterners.

6. Plains Indian culture was based on just three animals: the buffalo, the horse, and the longhorn cow.

7. The many wars among plains Indians tribes were mostly for control and ownership of land.

8. A permanent peace was foreign to the Indian's view of the world.

9. Railroad companies discouraged the slaughter of bison because they were a tourist attraction.

10. According to General Sheridan, Congress should strike a medal with "a dead buffalo on one side and a discouraged Indian on the other."

11. The black regiments ("buffalo soldiers") in the West had the lowest desertion rate and the lowest number of courts-martial of any western regiments.

12. "Custer's Last Stand" is now seen as a rare case of simple bad luck on Custer's part, since he was widely regarded as a cautious and careful commander who would not ordinarily have put his soldiers in such grave danger.

13. "Custer's Last Stand" was the last major Indian battle.

14. The Dawes Act represents the government's attempt to preserve and strengthen Indian tribes as a source of cultural identity.

15. The Dakota Sioux did not go to war with the whites until the end of the 1860s, but within a generation, the survivors had been herded onto the Pine Ridge Reservation, where in 1890 many of them were massacred.

16. Acre for acre, farmers won more of the West than any other pioneers.

17. The profits in cattle were so great that ranchers began to conserve grassland for future use.

18. Most of the so-called "cowtowns" had gun control laws to discourage drunken cowboys from disturbing the peace.

19. "Pulps" or "dime novels" were cheaply printed books priced at ten cents and bought mostly by boys in search of adventure.

20. Mining towns seldom were developed beyond a few wooden public buildings and hundreds of miners' tents before the gold or silver ran out, causing the towns to be abandoned.

III. Multiple Choice

1. Both the Navajo and the Pueblo Indians feared

a. the white man
b. the Apache tribe
c. starvation
d. diseases of the white man

2. The fuel used by the Plains Indians for cooking and warmth in a treeless land was

a. grass
b. coal from ground mines
c. wood brought from the Rockies
d. bison manure

3. Wholesale slaughter of bison began when

a. the work crews on railroads needed food
b. the Indians began to sell the horns
c. buffalo robes became fashionable
d. the repeater rifle was developed

4. Soldiers believed that the Indians' claim to land was not equal to the whites' because the Indians

a. did not use the land efficiently
b. were savages
c. did not need it at all
d. were nomads

5. The supporters of the Dawes Act argued that the Indians must be

a. put on reservations
b. Americanized
c. helped to keep their culture
d. forced to comply with army regulations

6. The reservation lands had been allotted to the Indians because

a. the land was not suitable for agriculture
b. easterners sympathized with the Indians' plight
c. they were promised farm land
d. the Spanish had granted them in special charters

7. Wovoka, a Paiute, built up a following by preaching that the white man would disappear if the Indians

a. fought back
b. migrated to Canada
c. adopted Christianity
d. performed a ritual dance

8. Which of the following was a provision of the Dawes Severalty Act of 1887?

a. Indian tribes were dissolved
b. each Indian head of a family would receive at least 160 acres of treaty land
c. remaining Indian lands could not be sold for 25 years
d. all of these.

9. A longhorn steer worth $5 in Texas could be sold in Kansas or Missouri, still on the hoof, for at least

a. $10
b. $15
c. $25
d. $125

10. In 1876, Wild Bill Hickok was shot dead in Deadwood, South Dakota during that frontier town's worst year for homicides. During the entire year, there were how many other homicides in Deadwood?

a. one
b. two
c. three
d. over 200, though no accurate count was kept.

IV. Fill-in

Fill in each blank in the following statements with the correct information.

1. The Census Bureau defined "settled" land as an area having an average population density of just _____ people per square mile.

2. Using that standard, _____ of the U.S. was unsettled at the time of the Civil War.

3. The Pony Express cut _____ days off the usual time it had taken to get a letter from Washington to Sacramento (via steamship and the Isthmus of Panama). The experiment lasted just _____ months, during which time the system made _____ transcontinental runs.

4. There may have been _____ million bison in 1800; by 1889 fewer than _____ survived.

5. One Comanche band of 2000 Indians had a herd of _____ horses.

6. With only _____ Native Americans roaming the Great Plains in 1860, war was not massive but it was chronic.

7. Of about 100,000 settled moving overland through Indian territory, only _____ were killed by Indians.

8. According to a quote attributed to General Sheridan, the only good Indian was a _____ Indian.

9. Between 1869 and 1876, the peak years of the fighting, the army recorded _____ "incidents" between the army and Indians.

10.   Where was "Custer's Last Stand"? _____

11.   The typical state of a surrendering tribe was near _____, with most of its young men _____.

12.   According to the Dawes Act, each Indian head of a family was to receive at least _____ acres of land, which would be his after _____ years.

13..   The Dawes Act intended for Indians to become _____.

14.   About _____ people, half of them women and children, were killed by soldiers guarding them at Wounded Knee Creek.

15.   In 1870, Americans were raising _____ million cattle; in 1900 the number had risen to _____ million

16.   In 1867, Joseph G. McCoy shipped _____ head of cattle from Abilene to Chicago. Four years later, _____ passed through several Kansas railhead towns on their way to America's dinner table.

17.   The end of the first cattle boom came with the great blizzard of _____; about _____ cowboys were killed and between _____ and _____ percent of the livestock died.

.18.   The King Ranch in Texas was as big as the state of _____.

19.   A steer that cost about $ _____ to raise could be driven to Kansas City or another railhead town for no more than $_____ and then sold for at least $ _____.

20.   Before the famous Comstock Lode ran out, it had yielded more than $_____ million in gold and silver.

V.   **Essay Questions**

Write notes under each of the following questions that would help you answer similar essay questions on an exam.

1.   Describe the American frontier of the late nineteenth century. Why was it considered of value in about 1870?

2.   What Indian groups lived in the West? Compare and contrast their styles of life. What does this indicate about our characterization of all Native Americans as having an "Indian culture"?

3.   Describe the life of the plains Indians. Should they have been led alone to roam the plains and to preserve their nomadic way of life? Explain.

4. What were the characteristics of the Indian wars? Were the wars inevitable or could responsible government action have prevented them? Explain.

5. Evaluate the Dawes Act of 1887. Was it an enlightened and realistic solution to the problems in the West? Why or why not?

6. What was the cattle kingdom? Include a description of the cowboy, the cattle drive, the economics involved, and the legends that grew from the descriptions of the cattle kingdom.

7. Describe the cowboy's life during a cattle drive. How does this differ from the image we have of cowboys?

8. Describe the mining frontier.

9. To what extent can it be said that people are affected as much by the legends of history as they are by the reality of history? Apply this idea to the era of the "opening" of the West. Is it helpful to explain the reality to those who believe the legend? Why or why not?

10. Would the word "exploitation" be an accurate one for the story told in this chapter? Why or why not? Would the use of the term "exploitation" represent a bias of the historian or a sound judgment from the reality of the times? Explain.

11. Read the quotation from Frederick Jackson Turner at the beginning of the chapter. Do you agree with Turner's analysis? Why or why not?

ANSWERS

II. True-False

1. True
2. True
3. False
4. True
5. True
6. False
7. False
8. True
9. False
10. True
11. True
12. False
13. False
14. False
15. True
16. False
17. False
18. True
19. True
20. False

III. Multiple Choice

1. b
2. d
3. c
4. a
5. b
6. a
7. d
8. d
9. c
10. c

IV. Fill-in

1. 2.5
2. half
3. 12; 18; 308
4. 30; 1,000
5. 15,000
6. 225,000
7. 350
8. dead
9. 200
10. Little Big Horn, Montana
11. starvation; dead
12. 160; 25
13. farmers (Americanized farmers)
14. 200
15. 23.8; 67.7
16. 35,000; 600,000
17. 1886; 300; 50%; 85%
18. Rhode Island
19. $5; $8; $25
20. $400

32

Stressful Times Down Home Agriculture, 1865-1896

*"When the Lawyer hangs around and the Butcher cuts a pound,
Oh the farmer is the man who feeds them all."*

"The aim of history, then, is to know the element of the present by understanding what came into the present from the past."

Frederick Jackson Turner

I. Key Words

You should be able to define the following words and explain their historical significance in relation to the development of American history.

subsistence and commercial agriculture
"Great American Desert"
dry farming
"rain follows the plow"
Great Plains
sod houses
Joseph Glidden
barbed wire
"nesters"
Oliver Evans
"Nebraska marble"
"Pap" Singleton
"Exodusters"
Nicodemus, Kansas
share tenants and sharecroppers
pellagra
crop-lien system
debt bondage
agrarianism
Henry W. Grady and the New South
James B. Duke
American Tobacco Company
"coffin nails"
Women's Christian Temperance Union
McGuffey's Readers
Patrons of Husbandry (Grange)

Southern Alliance(s)
co-ops
Granger laws
Mary Lease
gold, silver, and greenbacks
inflation and deflation; "cheap" money
Demonetization Act ("Crime of '73")
Bland-Allison Bill
"bimetallism" and "gold bugs"
Sherman Silver Purchase Act
People's Party (Populists)
popular (direct) election of senators
the secret ballot
initiative, recall and referendum
Panic of 1893
"free silver"
Jacob Coxey and "Coxey's Army"

II. True-False

If the statement is false, change any words necessary to make it true.

1. Farmers led the way on the western frontier, followed by cattlemen, miners, loggers, and soldiers.

2. Never in the history of the world have people put so much new land to the plow as quickly as Americans did in the final three decades of the 19th century.

3. Only about one homesteader in ten was a woman.

4. "Rain follows the plow" was the belief that moisture in the earth would be released by plowing the soil, and it would return to the earth as rainfall.

5. Except for cottonwood trees along the rivers, there were no trees on the Great Plains.

6. Barbed wire was the only major example of technology applied to farming on the Great Plains; once it was developed, all the problems of farming in the West were solved.

7. The typical farmer of the late 19th century was a long-term debtor whose real income (actual purchasing power) declined by century's end. Farm tenancy increased.

8. Only a few African Americans migrated to Kansas or other western states, and no trace remains today of their settlements.

9. Sharecropping was an economic system in which a farm laborer's rent increased in proportion to the amount of his harvest; if his crop doubled, so did his rent.

10. The 1890s American often viewed farmers as ridiculous people, hayseeds and yokels—characters to be mocked on the vaudeville stage.

11. There was a kind of security in the sharecropper system, in that the cropper who owed money was not likely to be evicted.

12. By 1890, Birmingham, Alabama, produced more pig iron than Pittsburgh.

13. Traditionalists to the core, farmers refused to let their wives have any significant role in the agrarian movement.

14. Though some farmers believed that overproduction was one cause of their problems, their only solution was to plant more crops, hoping that they could improve their income by sheer volume of output.

15. "Greenbacks" were government-printed Civil War paper dollars not redeemable in gold or silver, whose value fluctuated.

16. Inflation is particularly harmful to people (like farmers) who are in debt.

17. One problem with using silver as well as, or in place of, gold was that the price of silver was always changing, depending on how much silver was being mined in the West.

18. Tom Watson of Georgia proposed a political alliance between black and white farmers to save both races from financial despotism.

19. Most of the Populists' proposals for political reform eventually became law.

20. "Coxey's Army" was made up of unemployed men who marched on Washington in 1894, but Jacob Coxey himself was an eccentric millionaire.

III. Multiple Choice

1. According to Thomas Jefferson the "bone and sinew" of the Republic was

a. philosopher-kings
b. education
c. civil rights
d. the farmer

2. The pioneers refused to believe the warning of experts about the dryness of the plains and assumed that once the sod had been broken

a. the rainfall patterns would be altered
b. the ground would soak up moisture
c. moisture would seep up from below
d. crops would grow deeper roots

3. The efficient steel hedge that could be erected on the flimsiest of fenceposts was called

a. green steel
b. barbed wire
c. artificial wood
d. cattle stoppers

4. Which of these was *not* a characteristic of the sod house?

a. warm in winter
b. wet inside when it rained, since the roof was made of dirt
c. expensive to build, because of shipping costs
d. thick walls with deep windowsills and doorways

5. Farmers tended to see businessmen, bankers, landlords, editors, and politicians as

a. parasites
b. important: the farmers
c. Americans also
d. not trustworthy

6. In California, farmers clashed with miners because the miners

a. dug in their fields
b. lived an immoral life
c. polluted the rivers
d. grew richer than the farmers

7. The chief obstacle to farming on the Great Plains was

a. Indians
b. herds of bison
c. insects and blizzards
d. lack of water

8. Except for the western counties of Kansas and Nebraska, the worst off farmers in the nation were

a. along the West Coast
b. in the South
c. in the Northeast
d. in Missouri

9. Why did bankers and other creditors oppose the "free silver" idea?

a. silver would have inflated the economy, reducing the value of borrowed money
b. there was a nationwide scarcity of silver in the 1890s
c. they thought it was unfair for the government to give away silver, free of charge
d. gold was the only metal that had any real value

10. The most stable currency, according to financial conservatives, was

a. gold
b. silver
c. a combination of gold, silver, and paper money
d. "greenbacks"

IV. Fill-in Questions

Fill in each blank in the following statements with the correct information.

1. As of 1870, Americans had brought 408 million acres (1.6 million acres of new land annually) under cultivation, but by 1900 they had added _____ million acres (an average of _____ million acres each year).

2. By 1900, American farmers were producing up to _____ percent more corn and wheat than they had in 1870. Hog production went from _____ million in 1870 to _____ million in 1900.

3. In the eastern half the country (east of eastern Kansas), the annual rainfall was at least _____ inches, but in the "Great American Desert" it was only _____ or less.

4. The inventor of a machine that could mass-produce cheap and effective barbed wire was _____. By 1880, _____ million pounds had been sold.

5. One farmer without machinery took 50 to 60 hours to harvest _____ bushels of wheat per acre, but with machinery he could produce a larger crop with less than _____ hours per acre.

6. A single farmer could cultivate _____ times what his father could in the Civil War.

7. A crop that in 1872 brought the farmer $1,000 in real income was worth only $_____ in 1896.

8. In several western Kansas and Nebraska counties from 1889 to 1893, _____ out of 10 farmsteads changed hands.

9. Under the sharecropper system the landlord provided everything (except the labor) in return for _____ of the crop.

10. The price of a pound of cotton fell to _____ cents by the 1890s and during the depression of 1893, as low as _____ cents.

11. "Buck:" Duke spent $_____ on advertising in 1889; only the ready-to-eat _____ makers spent that much to promote their products.

12. Mary Lease said that farmers should raise less _____ and more _____.

13. In a standard speech describing a Georgia funeral, Henry Grady tried to promote southern industrialism by noting that the South had furnished for that funeral only the _____ and the _____.

14. During a period of deflation, prices and wages _____.

15. In 1865 there had been $_____ in circulation for every American, in 1878 there was $_____.

16. Between 1837 and 1873, the price of silver in the U.S. was legally pegged to the price of gold at a ratio of _____ to one. In 1873, the value of silver and gold mined was about equal, about $_____ million each.

17. The Sherman Silver Purchase Act of 1890 required the Treasury to purchase _____ million ounces of silver each month—the entire output of the nation's silver mines. In that year, the free-market price of silver had declined, so that an ounce of gold was worth _____ ounces of silver.

18. The most controversial of the Populists' demands was for the abolition of national banks and government ownership of _____ and the telegraph.

19. In 1892, the federal income tax rate was _____ percent for all.

20. The major obsession of the Populists was their demand for the unlimited coinage of silver, its value pegged to gold, a policy that was known as "_____."

V. Essay Questions

Write notes under each of the following questions that would help you answer similar essay questions on an exam.

1. What was the crisis of American agriculture between 1865 and 1900?

2. Explain the difference between subsistence and commercial agriculture. Why was the history of farming, especially in the West, a history of indebtedness?

3. Explain the belief that "rain follows the plow."

4. What was the historic reputation of the farmer? How and why did this change in the late 19th century?

5. Describe the construction of a sod house. What advantages and disadvantages did this construction material have?

6. Describe the innovations on American farms that resulted in such an increase in production. What was the relationship between changes in industrial production and this increase in farm production?

7. Was the share-tenant and the share-cropper system a realistic solution to a post-Civil War economic problems or merely a case of racism and landlord oppression? Explain.

8. What part did the world market play in the farmer's economic difficulties?

9. Describe the Grange and the co-op movement. Evaluate these as answers to the farmers' problems.

10. List and explain briefly the main parts of the Populist program.

11. Describe the money system and the relationship between paper money and gold or silver coins. What economic problems would exist today if the money supply were limited to the natural availability of gold and silver? What economic problems could happen when paper money is not based on precious metals or other things of tangible value? What is the U.S. dollar based on today?

12. Explain the silver issue. What were the government's efforts to solve the money problems? Is gradual inflation, deflation or stability of money and prices better for an economy? Explain who benefits under each condition.

13. Describe the development of industry in the New South.

ANSWERS

II. True-False

1. False
2. True
3. False
4. True
5. True
6. False
7. True
8. False
9. True
10. True
11. True
12. True
13. False
14. True
15. True
16. False
17. True
18. True
19. True
20. True

III. Multiple Choice

1. d
2. a
3. b
4. c
5. a
6. c
7. d
8. b
9. a
10. a

IV. Fill-in

1. 431; 14.4
2. 150%; 25; 63
3. 32; 16
4. Joseph Glidden; 80.5
5. 20; 10
6. six
7. $500
8. 9
9. half
10. six; five
11. $800,000; cereal
12. corn; hell
13. corpse; hole in the ground
14. drop or decrease
15. $31.18; $16.25
16. 16; $36
17. 4.5; 20
18. railroads
19. 2%
20. "free silver"

33

In the Days of McKinley
The United States as a World Power
1896-1903

"... you shall not press upon the brow of labor this crown of thorns, you shall not crucify mankind upon a cross of gold."

William Jennings Bryan

"The task of the historian is to understand the peoples of the past better than they understood themselves."

Butterfield

I. Key Words

You should be able to define the following words and explain their historical significance in relation to the development of American history.

William McKinley
Mark Hanna
William Jennings Bryan ("Boy Bryan")
"Cross of Gold" speech
Populists
fusionists
election of 1896
poll tax, literacy tests, and the "grandfather clause"
Booker T. Washington
Tuskegee Institute
the Atlanta Compromise
W.E.B. DuBois
imperialism
isolationism
Commodore Matthew Perry
"jingoism"
John Fiske and Josiah Strong
Our Country
Anglo-Saxonism
Alfred Thayer Mahan
The Influence of Sea Power upon History
Frederick Jackson Turner

"frontier thesis"
Cuban rebellion
the "yellow press"
William Randolph Hearst and Joseph Pulitzer
Valeriano ("The Butcher") Weyler
USS *Maine*
de Lome letter
"splendid little war"
George Dewey
"Rough Riders"
Tenth Negro Cavalry
Teller Amendment
American Anti-Imperialist League
colonialism and anti-imperialism
Philippine debate
"immune" regiments
Albert J. Beveridge
coaling stations
annexation of Hawaii
McKinley Tariff of 1890
Queen Liliuokalani
Sanford Dole
Philippine insurrection
Emilio Aguinaldo
Open Door policy
Boxer rebellion
Theodore Roosevelt
Roosevelt Corollary to the Monroe Doctrine
Panama Canal Zone
Philippe Bunau-Varilla
Republic of Panama
gunboat diplomacy and dollar diplomacy

II. True-False

If the statement is false, change any words necessary to make it true.

1. Mark Hanna was known as a spokesman for moderation and railed against exploitive capitalists and socialists alike.

2. William McKinley was ambitious, undignified, and largely untalented, but his personal charisma won him the election in 1896 anyhow.

3. "Boy" Bryan was actually too young to run for president, according to the Constitution.

4. William Jennings Bryan accepted the entire platform of the Populist Party, not just the "free silver" plank.

5. Before Bryan, presidential nominees had been quiet, as though it were an insult to the dignity of the office to woo votes.

6. More people voted for William Jennings Bryan than had voted for anyone elected president up to 1896, but he still lost the election.

7. Mark Hanna tried to persuade American voters that the Republican party was "the party of decency."

8. Despite poverty and sharecropping elsewhere in the South, by 1890, over 40% of black farmers in Virginia owned their own land, thanks to the demand for tobacco.

9. The problem with using literacy tests to decide who could vote in the South was that a fair literacy test would disfranchise just as many white voters as it would black voters (who were the intended target of the tests.)

10. Lynching was a particularly gruesome southern tradition, but they were rare after 1890 because of increasingly effective local and state prosecution of lynch mob leaders and participants.

11. Booker T. Washington's apparent acceptance of second-class citizenship for southern blacks made him popular among whites, but intensely disliked by his fellow southern blacks.

12. Neither the American people nor any of their leaders wanted anything to do with the scramble for colonies that engrossed Europe.

13. Teddy Roosevelt believed that nations needed to fight wars now and then in order to toughen up.

14. The Reverend Josiah Strong objected to American imperialism because he did not think that a Christian nation ought to govern non-Christian parts of the world.

15. A theory of history that fired up the expansionist movement was based on the announcement that the western frontier no longer existed.

16. American businessmen clamored for intervention in Cuba to protect their investments.

17. The Spanish navy set off a mine on February 15, 1898, which blew up the battleship USS *Maine*.

18. The U.S. acquired the Hawaiian Islands as part of the treaty ending the Spanish American War.

19. McKinley led the American people into overseas adventures that gave the nation something of an empire, though the U.S. was not isolated from world affairs before his presidency.

20. Mark Hanna celebrated the news that Theodore Roosevelt had become president after McKinley's assassination.

III. Multiple Choice

1. William McKinley was the Republican party's leading expert on

a. the tariff
b. winning elections
c. foreign policy
d. the money issue

2. Who said, "You shall not crucify mankind upon a cross of gold"?

a. Mark Hanna
b. William McKinley
c. William Jennings Bryan
d. Tom Watson

3. Most farmers whose condition was not desperate accepted the Republican contention that Bryan was

a. their candidate
b. a dangerous radical
c. pro-farmer and pro-labor
d. really a supporter of tight money

4. In his inaugural address, McKinley said that the United States had to "avoid the temptation of

a. war"
b. European involvement"
c. isolationism"
d. territorial expansion"

5. Josiah Strong argued that Americans had what duty regarding other lands and their peoples?

a. a racial and religious duty to spread American institutions by taking them over
b. an economic duty to help develop other nations so as to develop export markets
c. a moral duty to "live and let live"—he supported isolationism.
d. a duty to spread the Christian faith, but also to recognize that all peoples are equal.

6. Valeriano Weyler was called "The Butcher" for his repressive policies, which included the establishment of the first

a. medical experimental teams
b. use of torture
c. concentration camps
d. death squads

7. Commodore Dewey defeated the Spanish Fleet in Manila Bay but the did not invade Manila because

a. he had no troops aboard his ships
b. he had no order to do so
c. Filipino rebels were taking Manila
d. he was afraid of great loss of life

8. The Open Door policy was intended to protect access to the trade of which nation?

a. Cuba
b. Japan
c. China
d. Hawaii

9. Motives for American imperialism included

a. the writings of Josiah Strong
b. the writings of Alfred Thayer Mahan
c. Frederick Jackson Turner's comments on the closing of the frontier
d. all of these

10. According to Senator Albert Beveridge, should the U.S. take over and govern the Philippines?

a. Yes, because they were an inferior people
b. No, because it would be bad for trade
c. Yes, because it would expand American trade
d. No, because it would be against American religious principles

IV. Fill-in Questions

Fill in each blank in the following statements with the correct information.

1. William Jennings Bryan's main speaking topic for the four years prior to the election of 1896 was the free coinage of _____.

2. In 1896, William Jennings Bryan ran for president as the candidate of _____ political parties.

3. Bryan traveled more than _____ miles by train and delivered _____ speeches in 29 states in only 14 weeks.

4. During the election campaign of 1896, the Republican Party printed _____ pamphlets for every American voter.

5. _____ of the 15 biggest cities were controlled by Republican machines, and they delivered their votes to McKinley.

6. Four southern states (Alabama, Louisiana, North Carolina and Georgia) allowed a man to vote without paying a poll tax if his _____ had been eligible to vote before 1867.

7. Each year in the 1890s there were _____ lynchings, primarily in the South.

8. The best known of Booker T. Washington's critics was _____.

9. By 1870, American exports totaled $_____ million, mostly _____ products.

10. According to Alfred Thayer Mahan, a great nation must have a _____ if it is to be a great nation.

11. The historian Frederick Jackson Turner said in 1893 that the source of American democracy, social stability and prosperity was the _____ (which, ironically, according to the Census Bureau, was closed as of 1890.)

12. The American business community had substantial investments in Cuba, about $_____ million in railroads, mines, and sugar cane plantations.

13. On February 15, 1898, the battleship USS *Maine* exploded in Havana harbor with a loss of _____ sailors.

14. The United States Army in 1898 numbered _____ men, less than half the size of the army of _____.

15. More than _____ American soldiers died from typhoid, tropical diseases, and tainted meat, but only _____ were listed as killed in combat in the Spanish-American War.

16. Over _____ men served in the army in the period of the Spanish-American War and probably an equal number was turned down.

17. The army tried to prepare for jungle warfare by authorizing the recruitment of up to _____ "immunes," young men who were thought to be immune to tropical diseases.

18. About _____ blacks served in the war, 4,000 of them in the "immunes."

19. One motive for the American annexation of Hawaii was a two-cent-per-pound bounty on American-grown _____.

20. McKinley justified American rule over the Philippines by citing a duty to "Christianize" the islands; he did not realize that _____ out of five Filipinos were Roman Catholic, and _____ out of five Protestant.

21. More than _____ Americans died in the effort to pacify the Philippines.

22. The "Open Door" policy was an attempt to preserve the territorial integrity of _____.

23. An ocean voyage of 12,000 miles from San Francisco to Cuba, in the absence of the Panama Canal, took 67 days. The same voyage, once the Panama Canal was finished, was only _____ miles.

24. The idea of influencing Latin America by investment rather than armed force was called _____ diplomacy.

25. Every president from Theodore Roosevelt to _____ used troops to enforce American wishes in Latin America.

V. Essay Questions

Write notes under each of the following questions that would help you answer similar essay questions on an exam.

1. Describe the election of 1896's candidates, campaign, outcome, and significance in American political history. Were the innovations in this election beneficial to the American democratic system? Why or why not?

2. In what sense could it be said that Bryan was a man for the nineteenth century and McKinley a man for the twentieth?

3. Why did the Populists join the Democratic party for the 1896 election? What were the consequences of this action, for both parties?

4. In what ways was the U.S. not really isolationist in the nineteenth century? Is it possible to be isolationist and also industrialized? Explain.

5. List and explain briefly the causes of American imperialism in the late nineteenth century. Which cause or causes were most important? Why?

6. What arguments could be used to support or refute the ideas of Josiah Strong?

7. Explain why the United States became involved in the war with Spain. How might the war have been avoided?

8. Describe the "splendid little war." What part did the element of luck and coincidence play in the success of the United States?

9. What arguments were used in the debate over the annexation of the Philippines?

10. Trace the steps by which the U.S. acquired the Hawaiian Islands. Is this a case of the end justifying the means, or were the long-run beneficial consequences outweighed by the short-term abuse of power? Explain.

11. Describe the foreign policy principles and actions of Theodore Roosevelt.

12. How did the United States acquire the land for the Panama Canal?

ANSWERS

II. True-False

1. True
2. False
3. False
4. False
5. True
6. True
7. True
8. True
9. False
10. False
11. False
12. False
13. True
14. False
15. True
16. False
17. False
18. False
19. True
20. False

III. Multiple Choice

1. a
2. c
3. b
4. a
5. a
6. c
7. a
8. c
9. d
10. a

IV. Fill-in

1. silver
2. two
3. 13,000; 600
4. five
5. Fourteen
6. grandfather
7. 150
8. W.E.B. DuBois
9. $320; agricultural
10. navy
11. frontier
12. $50
13. 260
14. 28,000; Belgium
15. 5,000; 379
16. 274,000
17. 10,000
18. 10,000
19. sugar
20. four; one
21. 5,000
22. China
23. 4,000
24. dollar
25. Herbert Hoover

34

Theodore Roosevelt and the Good Old Days American Society in Transition, 1890-1917

"the strenuous life"

"You must remember that the president is about six years old."

"If one can really penetrate the life of another age, one is penetrating the life of one's own [age]."

T. S. Eliot

I. Key Words

You should be able to define the following words and explain their historical significance in relation to the development of American history.

"Gay Nineties"
"good old days"
Middle America (middle-class America)
Progressive era
Theodore Roosevelt
William McKinley
"the strenuous life"
Booker T. Washington
Morrill Land Grant Act of 1862
career-based education (compared to liberal arts education)
coeducational institutions
Plessy v. Ferguson (1896)
"agricultural and mechanical" schools
Tuskegee Institute
George Washington Carver
Samuel Langhorne Clemens (Mark Twain)
Henry James
realism and naturalism in literature
Frank Norris
Jack London
Nellie Bly (Elizabeth Cochran)
mass-circulation magazines
Carnegie libraries

Chautauqua movement and lyceums
Coney Island
Chicago World's Fair
Ferris wheel
cocaine
bicycle craze
League of American Wheelmen
John L. Sullivan
Jack Johnson

II.   True-False

If the statement is false, change any words necessary to make it true.

1. After 1890, European immigration practically ceased to be a reason for American population growth.

2. By the 1890s medicine had conquered, for the most part, typhoid, scarlet fever, strep throat, diphtheria, whooping cough, and measles.

3. The days that preceded the American intervention in the First World War have lived on in the national memory as the original "good old days."

4. The turn of the century was an important time because middle-class values and aspirations have dominated American culture in the twentieth century.

5. Increasingly well educated, the new middle class quietly supported the zealous, religious piety of their parents.

6. The economic success that was central to the "good old days" blinded well-to-do Americans to many social evils that afflicted the less fortunate.

7. Theodore Roosevelt believed that the president must be a good fellow and a showman; like the middle class of his time, he was confident, optimistic, and glad to be alive.

8. The foundation of middle-class vigor was higher education and an intangible factor best described as "character."

9. Institutions of higher education founded in the latter half of the 19th century included state universities and many colleges established by wealthy philanthropists.

10. "Agricultural and mechanical" colleges were founded (particularly in the South) to train blacks for manual occupations.

11. The two great novelists of the period, Mark Twain and Henry James, set most of their novels in Europe to show the difference between European and American culture.

12. In naturalistic writing, such as the works of Theodore Dreiser, the moralistic literary tradition required that poor people should be portrayed as more honest and ultimately happier than rich people, and sinful behavior must always be punished by the end of the book.

13. The female journalist who used the pen name "Nellie Bly" claimed she could go around the world in less time than the hero of Jules Verne's book *Around the World in Eighty Days*, but she failed.

14. The middle class of the antebellum period believed that constant work was the human fate, and idleness, such as casual travel, was a sin.

15. The Ferris wheel at the Chicago World's Fair in 1893 was 250 feet in diameter with 36 cars suspended around the wheel, each of which could carry 60 people. There has never been a larger Ferris wheel in all the years before or since.

16. Some amusement parks were built by trolley companies to promote more weekend use of streetcars.

17. There is no evidence, despite the legend, that Abner Doubleday drafted systematic rules for the sport of baseball.

18. Professional baseball became segregated by race only after the turn of the century.

19. Working-class people who could not afford the time or the money to attend sports events in person often followed their heroes in the sports pages of newspapers.

20. Jack Johnson, like Gentleman Jim Corbett and John L. Sullivan, the "Boston Strong Boy," was a source of pride for his fellow Irish immigrants.

III. Multiple Choice

1. 1900 seems a watershed year because a group brimming with confidence came into its own. This group was the

   a. farmers
   b. American middle class
   c. immigrants
   d. lower class workers

2. If you were a guest at Chautauqua, which of the following would you be most likely to do?

   a. ride a Ferris wheel
   b. listen to a lecture or a concert
   c. watch a horserace (and bet on the outcome)
   d. "take the cure" in a mineral bath

3. Historians have referred to the generation that lived before the First World War as the last to enjoy basking in an

a. age without problems
b. effort to remake the world
c. age of heroes and leaders
d. age of American innocence

4. Roosevelt shattered the image that had been nurtured by every president, that of

a. nonchalant aloofness
b. boisterous activity
c. soul-less dignity
d. a friend to the dispossessed

5. In dozens of articles and looks, Roosevelt wrote of the glories of

a. the cowboy life
b. history
c. warfare
d. the strenuous life

6. The writings of realists like Howells are sometimes lumped with romanticists and sentimentalism as the

a. romantic trash of the 90s
b. unrealistic dreamers
c. genteel tradition
d. gay 90s popular cultists

7. McClure and Munsey pioneered the curious but successful economics of selling their publications

a. for less than cost
b. by door to door salesmen
c. for twice the cost
d. through churches

8. Which of the following illustrate the changing status of women at the turn of the century?

a. Mary Lease
b. the telephone operator
c. the typist
d. all of these

9. The League of American Wheelmen was founded to promote

a. bicycling
b. electric cars
c. automobiles of any kind
d. roller skating

10. One spectator sport that actually declined during the "good old days" was

a. basketball
b. boxing
c. horse racing
d. boxing

IV. Fill-in Questions

Fill in each blank in the following statements with the correct information.

1. _____ million immigrants came to the United States between 1890 and 1910.

2. Life expectancy in 1900 for native-born white Americans was about _____ years.

3. Nationwide, compared to today, Americans were _____ times more likely to die from syphilis a century ago.

4. Theodore Roosevelt's personal motto was "Speak softly and carry a big _____.

5. According to the British ambassador, Roosevelt was about _____ years old.

6. At Harvard, Roosevelt took up _____ as a varsity sport.

7. Though he only did it once, and was criticized even so, Roosevelt invited _____ to lunch at the White House.

8. The foundation of middle-class vigor was _____.

9. In 1860 there were only about _____ free secondary schools in the U.S.; by 1915 there were _____.

10. The idea that students could pick and choose from a long list of courses to design their own elective curriculum was promoted by President Eliot at _____.

11. By 1910, when _____ percent of the U.S. population was illiterate (including recent immigrants), one black person in _____ above the age of 10 could neither read nor write.

12. Elizabeth Cochran went around the world in 1890 in _____ days.

13. By 1900, the combined circulation of the four largest American magazines totaled _____ million per month, more than all American magazines combined only 20 years earlier.

14. Before his death, Andrew Carnegie helped found _____ free public libraries.

15. An 1878 magazine article claimed that _____ was "the cure for young people afflicted with timidity in society."

16. Moralists condemned the sport of _____ because it could promote casual relations between young people of the opposite sex.

17. By 1900, almost _____ percent of clerical workers were female, up from _____ percent a decade earlier.

18. John L. Sullivan earned as much as $_____ a fight.

19. Often, elementary school teachers received no training and were miserably paid, about $_____ a year in rural states.

20. The trolley fare from downtown New York to Coney Island was _____ cents, with children riding free.

V. Essay Questions

Write notes under each of the following questions that would help you answer similar essay questions on an exam.

1. What people would not consider the 1890s the "good old days"? Why?

2. Describe Theodore Roosevelt. Was he a capable leader and president given his style of life? Why or why not?

3. What educational changes were brought about at the turn of the century? Include public schools and colleges in your description. What were the sources of problems or the failures of the system? Be specific.

4. Explain the literary concepts of realism and naturalism.

5. Describe the magazines of the period. What changes in magazines were indicators of the fixture? Does the increase in magazine readership indicate a decline in an interest in good literature? Explain.

6. Explain the development of Chautauqua. To what extent is it an "American" institution in its characteristics?

7. Describe the working class leisure-time activities. Could this be a first in history—fun, leisure, and enjoyment for the masses? Explain.

8. Describe the fitness craze and its relationship to the bicycle. Why is it a product of affluence and a machine-oriented society?

9. Was the office girl a forerunner to feminism or an opponent of feminist attitudes? Explain your viewpoint with evidence and arguments.

10. Describe the changes in the American office. How did these affect women? Were these changes beneficial or harmful to the advancement of women? Why?

11. Discuss the social and economic issues related to sports at the turn of the century. Which of these are still live issues today?

12. Describe the efforts of women to enhance their status and influence in American society in the late nineteenth century.

ANSWERS

II. True-False

1. False
2. False
3. True
4. True
5. False
6. False
7. True
8. False
9. True
10. True
11. False
12. False
13. False
14. True
15. False
16. True
17. True
18. True
19. True
20. False

III. Multiple Choice

1. b
2. b
3. d
4. c
5. d
6. c
7. a
8. d
9. a
10. c

IV. Fill-in

1. Twelve
2. 45
3. 60
4. stick
5. six
6. boxing
7. Booker T. Washington
8. wealth

9. 100; 12,000
10. Harvard University
11. 7.7%; three
12. 72
13. 2.5%
14. 2,800
15. cocaine
16. bicycling
17. 25%; 15%
18. $20,000
19. $200
20. 5 cents

35

Age of Reform
The Progressives

"I aimed at the nation's heart and hit it in the stomach."

Upton Sinclair

"Personally, I believe in woman's suffrage, but ... I do not regard it as a very important matter."

Theodore Roosevelt

"Historians ought to be precise, faithful, and unprejudiced; and neither interest, fear, hatred, nor affection, should make them swerve from the way of truth."

Cervantes

I.   Key Words

You should be able to define the following words and explain their historical significance in relation to the development of American history.

Progressives
Social Gospel
William Allen White
Louis Brandeis
W.E.B. DuBois
WASPs
Jane Addams
Herbert Croly
The Promise of American Life
Hammer v. Dagenhart
Niagara Movement
National Association for the Advancement of Colored People
W.E.B. DuBois
"talented tenth"
Brownsville incident
Frederick W. Taylor
"scientific management"
"Golden Rule" Jones
Lincoln Steffens
The Shame of the Cities
muckrakers

Ida Tarbell
McClure's
Upton Sinclair
The Jungle
city manager system
"Oregon system"
initiative, referendum, and recall
Robert "Fighting Bob" La Follette
"Wisconsin idea"
Hiram Johnson
Eugene Debs
Victor Berger
"sewer socialism"
American Federation of Labor
Samuel Gompers
"Wobblies"
Industrial Workers of the World
bindle stiffs, tramps, hobos, bums and "bulls"
"Big Bill" Haywood
Carrie Chapman Catt
National American Woman Suffrage Association
Charlotte Perkins Gilman
Alice Paul
"white slavery"
Margaret Sanger
Storyville
Mann Act
Prohibition
Carry Nation
Woman's Christian Temperance Union

II. True-False

If the statement is false, change any words necessary to make it true.

1. Only once in two centuries has the United States been shaken by a revolution, the secession of the southern states in 1861.

2. Few of the reforms of the early 20th century were original to the new century, but only during the Progressive Era were so many reforms so successful.

3. The progressives succeeded because their reforms appealed to a much larger and more broadly dispersed constituency than other reform groups.

4. In the context of American political history, the word "reform" has the same meaning as "revolution," and usually involved violence or threats to order.

5. Most progressive reformers were concerned with the welfare of those in the bottom ranks of society, but they also feared the masses

6. According to Herbert Croly in *The Promise of American Life*, the old Jeffersonian principle of "the less government the better" still applied to American society in the new century.

7. All, or nearly all of the progressives were anti-imperialists and isolationists, and most were afraid to go to war.

8. The NAACP was founded by progressive reformers, although improved race relations was not often a high priority in the progressive movement.

9. With the exception of "free silver," the progressives enacted most of the old Populist reform program early in the 20th century.

10. According to Lincoln Steffens, the "shame of the cities" was poverty.

11. Ida Tarbell was one of the best writers among the muckraking journalists, but the publisher of *McClure's* hired her to write an exposé of Standard Oil for his magazine because John D. Rockefeller had put his father out of business.

12. Upton Sinclair wrote *The Jungle* to promote socialism, but the books's popularity led to political reform, not revolution.

13. Robert LaFollette went beyond the negative, or regulatory, powers of government to create agencies that provided positive services for the people.

14. LaFollette disliked political machine methods and refused to use them in the cause of reform.

15. Most Progressives advocated municipal ownership of public utilities ("sewer socialism") but were otherwise staunchly antisocialist, fearing revolution from below..

16. Victor Berger of Milwaukee linked socialism and progressivism and preached class-based revolution against capitalism.

17. The union-labor movement grew during the Progressive Era, but by 1910 the American Federation of Labor's membership was still less than 10% of the nation's nonagricultural labor force.

18. Most articulate Americans, women as well as men, believed that woman's delicacy and fine moral sense dictated a separate sphere from men.

19. Even where prostitution was normally illegal, it was common to tolerate houses that were discreetly operated.

20. The Mann Act was written to protect women from being lured into prostitution.

III. Multiple Choice

1. The progressive reformers were drawn from, and chiefly appealed to

   a. the urban underclass
   b. the urban middle class
   c. the urban and suburban upper class
   d. small-town and rural society

2. As a group, the progressives were

   a. economically comfortable
   b. well educated
   c. optimists
   d. all of these

3. The heart of the progressive constituency was the new class that had been created by

   a. industrialization
   b. philanthropy from the wealthy
   c. hard work ("rags to riches")
   d. successful labor unions

4. Most progressive leaders were
   a. Jewish
   b. recent immigrants
   c. WASPs
   d. not particularly interested in politics

5. Most of the progressive reformer mayors elected in the early 20th century

   a. were ousted from office after a year or two
   b. were unknown outside their communities
   c. were socialists
   d. were elected to office because of public disgust with municipal corruption.

6. The "shame of the cities," according to Lincoln Steffens's articles in *McClure's*, was

   a. political corruption
   b. poverty
   c. poor housing, sanitation, and transportation
   d. racial discrimination and segregation

7. Upton Sinclair claimed that he "aimed at the nation's heart and hit it in the

a. head"
b. stomach"
c. breadbasket"
d. feet"

8. William S. U'ren persuaded a state legislature to adopt the initiative, recall, referendum, and the first primary law. That state was

a. Oregon
b. Pennsylvania
c. Delaware
d. California

9. To more radical members of Victor Berger's party, Berger's socialism was

a. too extreme for Americans
b. "sewer socialism"—city ownership of local utilities
c. a compromise with capitalists
d. not practical

10. The main difference between a hobo or "bindle stiff," and a tramp or bum was whether a man

a. was homeless
b. was an alcoholic or drug addict
c. earned his own living by honest work
d. had a criminal record, or was accused of being a criminal

11. Frederick W. Taylor, not a politician, is an example of progressivism in the form of

a. race relations
b. engineering efficiency
c. honest municipal government
d. temperance

12. Most of the middle-class suffragists argued that women should have the right to vote because they were

a. equal to men
b. citizens of the United States
c. more moral than men
d. human beings the same as men

13. *The Jungle* became a best-seller and led to

a. passage of a federal meat-inspection law
b. prohibition of liquor sales on Sundays
c. greater popularity for Socialists in the 1906 election
d. abolition of all radical labor unions

14. The most enduring and successful labor union in the early 20th century was

a. the American Federation of Labor
b. the Noble and Holy Order of the Knights of Labor
c. the Industrial Workers of the World ("Wobblies")
d. none of these

15. Apart from the struggle against prostitution, the most conspicuous moral crusade of the Progressive Era was

a. education
b. prohibition of alcohol
c. birth control
d. women's rights (other than voting)

IV. Fill-in Questions

Fill in each blank in the following statements with the correct information.

1. Most progressive reformers were white, old-stock Americans; these mostly Protestant, well-educated people would later be called _____.

2. Almost all progressives believed that the key to improving America was a powerful _____.

3. By 1907 about _____ of the states, governed or influenced by progressives, forbade the employment of children under _____ years of age.

4. W.E.B. DuBois believed that the "_____ tenth" of the black population would lead the race to progress and civil equality in the United States.

5. After Lincoln Steffens published *The Shame of the Cities*, more than _____ politicians and prominent Missouri businessmen were indicted for bribery and perjury. Elsewhere, _____ of reform mayors were elected after 1904 because of Steffens's work.

6. David Graham Phillips described the United States Senate as a kind of _____ club.

7. During the first decade of the century, no fewer than _____ articles and books of exposure were published.

8. The ten leading muckraking journals had a combined circulation of _____ million, not counting those who read the publications in libraries or barbershops.

9. Published in book form after first appearing in a Socialist magazine, *The Jungle* sold _____ copies and led to the passage of a federal _____-inspection law.

10. The "Wisconsin idea" linked state government with the state _____.

11. In 1904, _____ ran for president on the Socialist party ticket; all told, he would run _____ times.

12. Membership in the AFL reached _____ million in 1910, but the total nonagricultural labor force was almost _____ million.

13. Known as "_____" for their often violent behavior outside the law, railroad police tried to keep nonpaying passengers off freight trains.

14. Before the Constitution was amended to allow women throughout the U.S. to vote, _____ western states had already established that right.

15. Storyville was a legendary vice district in _____ until it was shut down in 1917.

V. Essay questions

Write notes under each of the following questions that would help you answer similar essay questions on an exam.

1. What was the background of and the characteristics of progressives? Why were the reformers not from the working or lower classes?

2. Describe the concept of statism and explain the many and varied viewpoints of people who called themselves progressives.

3. What were the varied roots of the progressives? Which root was the most important? Why?

4. Describe the muckrakers. Could reform have been accomplished without their help? Explain.

5. What ideas for the responsive and efficient operation of government were put into action by the progressives?

6. Explain Bob LaFollette's Wisconsin idea. To what extent was he acting on a political level the way industrialists were acting in the economic sphere? Explain.

7. Describe the Socialist movement at the turn of the century.

8. Explain the activities, goals, and problems of the Wobblies. Why did they not get middle-class support?

9. What was the relationship between women and the progressive movement? What problems did women face? Are these problems and attitudes of contemporary importance? Explain.

10. What were the arguments for and against prohibition? Why were women involved in the temperance movement?

11. Describe the major events in the life of Victor L. Berger. Should he be considered a significant American leader or a failure? Explain.

12. Explain why the Populists failed to get their program enacted, but within two decades, the Progressives had successfully made most of the same ideas into law.

13. Compare and contrast the labor philosophies of Eugene Debs and Samuel Gompers.

14. Today, it is generally assumed that reformers will favor better race relations. Explain why most of the Progressives put a far lower priority on racial equality than is acceptable in today's society.

15. How much of the progressive reform program is still part of the American legal system?

ANSWERS

II. True-False

1. True
2. True
3. True
4. False
5. True
6. False
7. False
8. True
9. True
10. False
11. False
12. True
13. True
14. True
15. True
16. False
17. True
18. True
19. True
20. True

III. Multiple Choice
1. b
2. d
3. a
4. c
5. d
6. a
7. b
8. a
9. b
10. c
11. b
12. c
13. a
14. a
15. b

IV. Fill-in questions

1. WASPs
2. government
3. two-thirds; 14
4. talented
5. 30; hundreds
6. millionaires'
7. 2,000
8. 3
9. 100,000; meat
10. university
11. Eugene Debs
12. 1.5; 20
13. "bulls"
14. six
15. New Orleans

36

Standing at Armageddon
The Progressives in Power
1901-1916

"How I wish I wasn't a reformer.... But I suppose I must live up to my part."

Theodore Roosevelt

"If we have done anything wrong, send your man to my man and we can fix it up."

J. P. Morgan to Roosevelt

"Every force has its form."

Shaker motto

I.   Key Words

You should be able to define the following words and explain their historical significance in relation to the development of American history.

"malefactors of great wealth"
the "Four Hundred"
Northern Securities Company
J. P. Morgan
United States Steel Company
Tennessee Coal and Iron Company
United Mine Workers
George F. Baer
John Mitchell
"Square Deal"
Alton B. Parker
Eugene V. Debs
Hepburn Act of 1906
Interstate Commerce Commission
Pure Food and Drug Act
Meat Inspection Act
John Muir
Sierra Club
Gifford Pinchot
National Forest Reserve

Mann Act of 1911 ("White Slave Traffic Act")
William Howard Taft
William Jennings Bryan
Dingley Tariff and Payne-Aldrich Tariff
Sixteenth Amendment
New Nationalism
Progressive (Bull Moose) Party of 1912
Woodrow Wilson
New Freedom
Underwood-Simmons Tariff
Louis Brandeis
Federal Reserve Act of 1913
Clayton Antitrust Act of 1914
Federal Trade Commission
Keating-Owen Act
Adamson Act

II. True-False

If the statement is false, change any words necessary to make it true.

1. Theodore Roosevelt was a member of an older American elite that was being elbowed aside by the industrial new rich of the late 19th century.

2. From the start, Roosevelt was determined to be his own man. Upon becoming president when McKinley was assassinated, he dismissed all of McKinley's cabinet.

3. Roosevelt did not fear competence among his subordinates, but was happy to delegate responsibility, because there was no doubt as to who was in charge.

4. Roosevelt recognized the energies and organizational skills of the industrial capitalists and thus decided to defer to their judgment on matters of business practice.

5. In any conflict between business and labor, Roosevelt (despite the nickname of "trustbuster") could always be counted on to side with business.

6. In the 1904 election, Roosevelt favored a lower tariff and a slightly inflationary money policy, both of which meant there was significant opposition to his renomination.

7. There was a distinct possibility that Debs, the Socialist candidate, might actually win the presidential election, since he got 400,000 votes in 1904.

8. Roosevelt set out to co-opt the socialists by eliminating many of the abuses that gave them their appeal.

9. Some of the biggest meat packers supported federal inspection of their factories, since they could more easily comply with sanitation laws than smaller companies could, thus giving them a competitive advantage.

10. Proportionate to total population, there may have been more drug addicts in the U.S. at the beginning of the 20th century than there are today.

11. The conservationist John Muir founded the Sierra Club in 1892 and helped establish Yosemite as a national park.

12. Though the idea of a National Forest Reserve dates back to 1891, Roosevelt set aside much more land than the three presidents before him had.

13. The common definition of prostitution early in the 20th century was the sale of sexual services in exchange for money.

14. William Howard Taft, Roosevelt's hand-picked successor, was a man remarkably like Roosevelt in appearance, temperament, and commitment to the "strenuous life."

15. Taft loved politics and would have won the nomination for the presidency, in 1908 even without Roosevelt's support.

16. Because of the high tariff, farmers paid higher prices for manufactured goods and suffered from decreased sales of agriculture products abroad.

17. As a conservationist, Roosevelt was careful to take only photographs when he went on an extended trip to East Africa after leaving office.

18. Woodrow Wilson won the 1912 election without getting more than 50% of the vote. Taft, the incumbent president, got less than a quarter of the popular vote.

19. The Federal Reserve System controls the rate of interest that banks must pay to borrow money, thus controlling economic policy for the nation.

20. With the Clayton Antitrust Act of 1914 and the establishment in the same year of the Federal Trade Commission to supervise the activities of trusts, Wilson was simultaneously following both his own New Freedom campaign theme of 1912 and the New Nationalism of Roosevelt.

III. Multiple Choice

1. The men chosen by Roosevelt to make up his cabinet and to work in subordinate roles were

   a. competent
   b. political hacks
   c. all McKinley-Hanna men
   d. loyal to him but incompetent

2. George Baer, leader of the mine operators, told the press that he would not deal win the UMW because his control over mines had been entrusted to him by

a. his father and grandfather
b. the laws of nature
c. the people of the United States
d. God

3. The big winner in the compromise of the mine-workers and owners was

a. the owners
b. Roosevelt
c. the workers
d. the Socialists

4. Roosevelt believed that what constituted real power in the presidency was

a. being morally right
b. having the police and army
c. being friends with the worker
d. personal popularity

5. In 1906 Congress passed an act that held which of the following responsible for those who suffered injuries on the job?

a. employees
b. railroads
c. government
d. unions

6. In 1902 the gigantic Coca Cola Company of Atlanta had to come up with a substitute for the "kick," in its beverage from

a. cocaine
b. carbonated water
c. caffeine
d. cocoa

7. The conservatives got a higher tariff in 1910 but agreed to a two percent corporate income tax and a

a. end to trusts
b. quota system on agricultural imports
c. recognition of unions
d. personal income tax

8. Which of these candidates was *not* on the ballot in 1912?

a. Woodrow Wilson
b. Eugene Debs
c. William Howard Taft
d. Louis Brandeis

9. The difference between "good" trusts and "bad" trusts, according to Roosevelt, was

a. the size of the trust
b. whether the trust's owners were in Roosevelt's social circle
c. whether the trust was organized by J. P. Morgan
d. vague—Roosevelt was inconsistent—but usually the behavior of the trust, not its size

10. How did Roosevelt weaken the Socialists?

a. by ordering the arrest of their leaders
b. by siding with industrial capitalists in every labor dispute
c. by reforming the economic system to eliminate abuses
d. by deporting Eugene Debs as an "undesirable citizen"

IV. Fill-in Questions

Fill in each blank in the following statements with the correct information.

1. Mrs. Astor's list of "acceptable" old-money New York families was the "_____."

2. As president, Roosevelt initiated 40 antitrust suits, of which he won ____ .

3. The 140,000 anthracite workers who went on strike in 1902 wanted a _____ percent increase in pay and an _____ -hour day.

4. The compromise in the mine workers strike of 1902 ended with a _____ percent pay raise and a _____ -hour day.

5. J. P. Morgan, despite being stung by Roosevelt in the Northern Securities case, donated $_____ to Roosevelt's campaign.

6. Roosevelt won _____ percent of the popular vote and won in the electoral vote _____ to 140, the greatest margin of victory since Grant won in 1872.

7. Eugene Debs won _____ votes in 1904, which amounted to only ____% of the total vote, but it was a _____ increase over his vote in 1900.

8. William Howard Taft weighed _____ pounds; his only form of exercise was _____.

9. While on safari in Africa, Roosevelt killed over _____ game animals, many of which he had stuffed to decorate his home on Long Island.

10. Roosevelt's 1912 campaign theme of proposals for reform, announced in 1910, was the _____.

11. The popular name for Roosevelt's Progressive party in 1912 was the _____ party.

12. Woodrow Wilson won the 1912 Democratic nomination, but only on the _____ ballot.

13. Wilson won _____ percent of the popular vote in 1912; Debs won _____ percent, and Taft won _____ percent.

14. The highest income tax bracket (for persons making over $500,000) was _____ percent. Those who earned less than $4,000 a year paid _____ income tax.

15. The Adamson Act required interstate railroads to put their workers on an _____ hour day.

V. Essay Questions

Write notes under each of the following questions that would help you answer similar essay questions on an exam.

1. Describe the trust-busting of Theodore Roosevelt. Although his record statistically was not as good as that of Taft, is the fact that he initiated the process on a large scale important? Explain.

2. What was the impact of Roosevelt on the coal strike of 1902? Was his threat to use troops a real one or a bluff? Explain. Did the workers or the owners win? Why?

3. Explain the Hepburn Act and the Pure Food and Drug Acts. To what extent did they begin a trend of regulation that is still controversial in American history?

4. Describe Roosevelt's conservation program. Was this perhaps the greatest legacy of Roosevelt? Why?

5. What were the weaknesses of Taft as president in approaches to issues and decisions?

6. Describe the candidates, issues, results, and significance of the election of 1912.

7. If Roosevelt and Wilson had not been presidents in 16 of the first 20 years of the twentieth century might there have been a trend to socialism? Explain.

8. What was Wilson's tax program? Was the corporate and personal income tax, proportionately higher for the rich, a fair system of taxation? Explain.

9. Describe the New Freedom program of Wilson. Was this intervention of the federal government in banking, farming, corporate liability, and employment a step in the right direction or an infringement on the rights of citizens in a free enterprise system? Explain.

ANSWERS

II. True-False

1. True
2. False
3. True
4. False
5. False
6. False
7. False
8. True
9. True
10. True
11. True
12. True
13. False
14. False
15. False
16. True
17. False
18. True
19. True
20. True

III. Multiple Choice

1. a
2. d
3. b
4. d
5. b
6. a
7. d
8. d
9. d
10. c

IV. Fill-in Questions

1. "Four Hundred"
2. 25
3. 20%; eight
4. 10%; nine
5. $150,000
6. 57.4%; 336
7. 400,000; 3%; fourfold
8. 300; golf
9. 3,000
10. New Nationalism
11. Bull Moose
12. 46th
13. 41.9%; 6%; 23.2%
14. 7%; no
15. eight

278

37

Over There
The United States and the First World War
1914-1918

"cooling off periods"
"strict accountability"
"We are going to war on the command of gold."

George Norris

"History repeats itself. That's one of the things wrong with history."

Clarence Darrow

I. Key Words

You should be able to define the following words and explain their historical significance in relation to the development of American history.

moral diplomacy
William Jennings Bryan
"cooling-off" period
Pancho Villa
John J. Pershing
Central Powers
Allied Powers
Kaiser Wilhelm II
Great War
anglophiles
Schlieffen Plan
"Huns"
poison gas
trench warfare
Battle of the Somme
economic warfare
U-boats
John Holland and Simon Lake
"strict accountability"
Lusitania
unrestricted submarine warfare
Sussex Pledge

"He Kept Us Out of War"
"preparedness" campaign
"peace without victory" and "peace among equals"
Verdun
Kultur
"the rape of Belgium"
Edith Cavell
Zimmermann note
William S. Sims
convoy system
destroyers
"Tin Lizzie" (Model T Ford)
American Expeditionary Force (AEF)
Vladimir Lenin
Treaty of Brest-Litovsk
Belleau Wood and the St.-Mihiel Salient
Sergeant Alvin York

II. True-False

If the statement is false, change any words necessary to make it true.

1. Wilson believed that the United States was unique among nations, and could act toward other countries in accordance with principles, not self-interest.

2. William Jennings Bryan, a Christian pacifist, believed that war was never justified under any circumstance.

3. Wilson had criticized Teddy Roosevelt's gunboat diplomacy, though as president he was not as unlike Roosevelt as both men thought.

4. Wilson was raised to believe in the superiority of the white race and found it difficult to act as an equal in dealing with the Japanese and Latin Americans.

5. When Francisco Madero, the idealistic leader of the Mexican revolution gained power, Americans took a hands-off policy and let the revolution take its course.

6. The United States intervened directly into Mexico's civil war in 1914.

7. While accomplishing nothing with Pershing's excursion, Wilson succeeded in alienating every political faction in Mexico.

8. For a generation before 1914 European rulers had filled the air with words of peace and conciliation.

9. As if they knew that the 1914 war would be only one of several to come, Europeans began to use the term "World War I to name the war almost as soon as it began.

10. Wilson was an anglophile, and many old-stock Americans were sympathetic to France, our "oldest friend."

11. Socialist Jews in New York hated Russia above all other countries, because of the czar's secret police, and many Irish-Americans hated Great Britain.

12. The German plan for defeating France was to knock the French army out of the war in six weeks. With almost no resistance on Germany's western front after August 1914, the plan worked as anticipated.

13. Most wartime trade was between the United States and Britain and France, with relatively little trade between the U.S. and Germany.

14. Though the Germans made it a critical part of their naval strategy, the modern submarine was actually an American invention.

15. The moral problem with unrestricted submarine warfare was that the design of submarines made it almost impossible for them to follow the traditional rules for war at sea, which required warning before ships could be attacked.

16. Henry Ford thought he could stop the war by sending a chartered shipload of pacifists, feminists, and reformers to Europe. The effort failed.

17. Woodrow Wilson narrowly won reelection in 1916 by running on the slogan "He Kept Us Out of War."

18. Germany calculated that the resumption of unrestricted submarine warfare would bring the United States into the war, but the war would be over before that intervention could affect the outcome of the war.

19. The Zimmerman telegram, a coded message sent from the German foreign minister to the Mexican government, proposing a wartime alliance (a message intercepted and decoded by British intelligence) was a foolish proposal, since Mexico was in no position to make war against the U.S.

20. In 1917 the Germans were proved right in gambling that American reinforcements could not turn the tide. By late 1918 they were proved wrong.

III. Multiple Choice

1. Wilson believed that the United States should act towards other nations not out of narrow self-interest but in accordance with

   a. power
   b. their best interests
   c. principles
   d. the defense of the continent

2. Bryan believed nations should wait and talk one year, in the event of a dispute, before

   a. declaring war
   b. negotiating
   c. going to the World Court
   d. calling for arbitration

3. Wilson raised no objections to a California state law that restricted the right of Japanese-Americans to

   a. emigrate back to Japan
   b. own land
   c. spread to the east
   d. carry weapons

4. Many factors caused war in Europe in 1914 including the weakness of the Czar, the irresponsibility of the Kaiser, the obligations of treaties, and

   a. Woodrow Wilson's attitude toward Europe
   b. the trade war
   c. the spread of communism
   d. a reckless arms race

5. Wilson called upon Americans to be neutral in

   a. diplomatic talks with the belligerent powers
   b. any and all economic dealings with Europe
   c. relations with Germany, but not with relations with Britain or France
   d. "fact as well as in name…in thought as well as action"

6. Because Britain had crushed a rebellion in Ireland in 1916, many Irish-Americans supported

   a. the British
   b. the Germans
   c. the Scotch Irish
   d. neither side

7. Admiral Sims insisted that merchant ships, guarded by small, fast, heavily armed destroyers, travel

a. at top speed
b. in convoys
c. only at night
d. along the shores of Newfoundland

8. According to the text, the most effective and deadly weapon of the war was the

a. airplane
b. tank
c. machine gun
d. poison gas

9. Wilson's slogan in the 1916 election was

a. "He Kept Us Out of War"
b. "Remember the *Lusitania*"
c. "Peace Without Victory"
d. "Stop the Merchants of Death"

10. The nation which suffered the lowest number of casualties in World War I was

a. Russia
b. Germany
c. France
d. the United States

IV. Fill-in Questions

Fill in each blank in the following statements with the correct information.

1. Americans alone owned $_____ billion in property in Mexico in 1911 including most of the railroads and _____ percent of the oil wells.

2. Wilson was surprised that ordinary Mexicans joined the fight against American intervention, an involvement which cost more than _____ lives in Vera Cruz.

3. Wilson ordered General John J. Pershing and _____ troops to capture the bandit guerrilla _____.

4. By 1917 Great Britain owed American lenders $_____ billion but Germany managed to borrow only $_____ million.

5. Historically minded Americans remembered _____ as America's "oldest friend."

6. One American in _____ was either foreign-born or a first generation citizen, many of them pro-German or unfriendly toward Britain.

7. Most German immigrants had come to the U.S. for _____ reasons, which meant that they did not hate their former homeland in the way that political or religious refugees might.

8. The _____ Plan, the basis of German strategy, was based on the assumption that Germany would have to fight a _____-front war.

9. The American regiment that spend the most time an the fighting front in WWI was the all-black _____ Infantry.

10. The entrenchments and earthworks called _____ that faced each over across "no man's land" stretched _____ miles in France and Belgium.

11. By the time the Battle of the Somme sputtered to a meaningless end, losses by the allies were at _____, with the British having lost _____ killed and wounded on the first day of battle.

12. Neutral Denmark, which never purchased American lard, imported _____ tons for resale to Germany.

13. American trade with the Allies climbed from $_____ million in 1914 to $_____ billion in 1916, a _____ increase in just two years.

14. The sinking of the *Lusitania* cost _____ lives, _____ of them American, but it was carrying _____ cases of small arms, which Germany publicized in an effort to defuse British and American assertions that the sinking of the ship was a violation of international law..

15. In 1915, a year after Europeans had gone to war, the United States had an army of just _____ men; 16 nations of the world had larger armies, and American artillery had only enough ammunition for _____ days of war.

16. Wilson's mediation plan, announced to Congress in January 1917, called for a "peace without _____."

17. By early 1917, Germany had _____ U-boats, and calculated that a resumption of unrestricted submarine warfare could _____ the British into submission before any American forces could enter the war.

18. _____senators and _____ representatives voted against entry into the war.

19. In April 1917, the month the U.S. entered the war, U-boats sank almost _____ tons of merchant shipping, and Britain had only a _____ supply of food on hand. For the war as a whole, U-boats sank _____ ships.

20. In 1900, 30 companies manufactured _____ automobiles; in just its first year of its production (1908), Henry Ford sold _____ Model Ts for $_____ each. By the end of its production in 1927, Ford had made _____ million Model Ts, and the price for a new one was just $_____.

21. Sergeant _____ won fame (and the Congressional Medal of Honor) in 1918 by single-handedly killing _____ Germans with _____ bullets and capturing _____ prisoners.

22. Over _____ million Americans were drafted and _____ million went to France; over _____ died, more than half from _____.

23. _____ percent of the French military forces were casualties (dead, wounded, missing or taken prisoner); the percentage for Russian troops was comparable.

24. Almost _____ million British soldiers died in WWI, and _____ million Frenchmen.

25. The nation having the highest number (not percentage) of casualties was _____.

V. Essay Questions

Write notes under each of the following questions that would help you answer singular essay questions on an exam.

1. Explain Wilson's attitude toward diplomacy—moral diplomacy and the missionary mind. Was his attitude in keeping with the American tradition or just his personal approach? Explain.

2. Describe the United States' intervention in Mexico. Was Wilson morally correct in his decisions? Why? Can one be morally correct and still have the outcome counterproductive? Explain.

3. Why did Europe go to war in 1914? Which do you consider the most important reason? Why?

4. What were Americans' views of the outbreak of war in Europe? Were we correct in our analysis? Explain.

5. What were the obstacles to a policy of neutrality? Would the United States have been better off to enter the war in the beginning and thereby end the war sooner? Why or why not?

6. Describe the deadly stalemate in Europe and how the new technology of warfare contributed to the stalemate.

7. Explain the blockade, freedom of the seas, and the war at sea. In what way was there no real solution to the dilemma facing Wilson regarding ships crossing the Atlantic? Why was submarine warfare immoral, in Wilson's view? What was the difference between submarine warfare and conventional naval weapons and tactics?

8. Describe the election of 1916. What was Wilson's theme? How accurate was the slogan Wilson used in that campaign?

9. List and explain briefly the reason for the American decision to go to war in 1917.

10. Describe the American contribution to the war in Europe. Is it fair to say that the American intervention won the war for the allies?

11. Given what we know now about how warfare has evolved since 1915, why was the submarine so controversial a weapon?

ANSWERS

II. True-False

1. True
2. False
3. True
4. True
5. False
6. True
7. True
8. False
9. False
10. True
11. True
12. False
13. True
14. True
15. True
16. True
17. True
18. True
19. True
20. True

III. Multiple Choice

1. c
2. a
3. b
4. d
5. d
6. b
7. b
8. c
9. a
10. d

IV. Fill-in

1. $2; 60%
2. 400
3. 6,000; Pancho Villa
4. 2.3; 27
5. France
6. three
7. economic
8. Schlieffen; two-
9. 369th
10. trenches; 475
11. 600,000; 60,000
12. 11,000
13. 825; 3.2; fourfold
14. 1,198; 139; 4,200
15. 108,000; two
16. victory
17. 100; starve
18. Six; 50
19. 900,000; three-week; 5,408
20. 8,000; 10,000; $825; 15; $290
21. Alvin York; 17; 17; 132
22. Three; 2; 100,000; disease
23. 75%
24. 1; 1.4
25. Russia

38

Over Here
World War I at Home, 1917-1920

"clear and present danger"

"In war, the first casualty is truth."

"When I try to understand what is happening today or try to decide what will happen tomorrow, I look back. A page of history is worth a volume of logic."

Oliver Wendell Holmes

I. Key Words

You should be able to define the following words and explain their historical significance in relation to the development of American history.

Great War
doughboys
Aircraft Production Board
Conscription Act
Shipping Board
United States Railway Administration
War Industries Board
Bernard Baruch
Herbert Hoover
"victory gardens"
"Hooverizing" America
wheatless Mondays, meatless Tuesdays
Selective Service Act
Samuel Gompers
National War Labor Board
369th Regiment
National American Woman Suffrage Association
Nineteenth Amendment
Lever Act
Eighteenth Amendment
Prohibition
Socialist Party of America
Victor Berger

Eugene Debs
Industrial Workers of the World
Espionage and Sedition Acts
Schenck v. United States (1919)
"clear and present danger" doctrine
American Civil Liberties Union (ACLU)
Committee on Public Information
George Creel
Flu pandemic
"Four-Minute Men"
"liberty cabbage"
Fourteen Points
League of Nations
"Big Four" at Versailles
Georges Clemenceau
Lloyd George
Vittorio Orlando
Article 10
Henry Cabot Lodge
Warren G. Harding
"normalcy"

II. True-False

If the statement is false, change any words necessary to make it true.

1. The First World War was simultaneously the apogee of progressivism and the undoing of progressivism.

2. The original Conscription Act (modified later) exempted men under 21 from the draft.

3. During the war, American industry and agriculture were regulated, indeed regulated as never before.

4. Government management of the nation's railroads during the war showed the folly of having bureaucrats, rather than businessmen, run a critical industry.

5. Hoover disagreed with Carnegie that wealthy men had special responsibilities to society and had no particular ambition to public or political service.

6. Hoover was a well-meaning but naïve humanitarian who failed or refused to apply his engineering skills to human problems.

7. As in Europe during the war, the national mobilization of the American economy meant rationing of food, fuel, and other critical resources needed by the armed forces.

8. In contrast to the Civil War experience with conscription, in WWI it was not possible for a man to hire a substitute or buy his way out of the draft.

9. The virtual capture of the national government's war offices by big business meant that organized labor's representatives had no voice in federal production policy, and wages remained stagnant.

10. Proportionately, more blacks than whites were in military uniform in WWI.

11. In direct contrast to what would happen in the next world war, women saw few changes in work or other areas of life during WWI.

12. Women would be allowed to vote, according to the 19th Amendment, only if they had served in the war in some capacity.

13. The federal government's persecution and prosecution of the IWW was entirely due to the union's opposition to WWI.

14. It was illegal to make a joke about a government official, a soldier, or the American flag, according to the Espionage Act of 1917 and the Sedition Act of 1918.

15. Worldwide, twice as many people died of the "Spanish flu" than were killed in WWI.

16. American consumer products, streets, even entire towns having German names were renamed during the war.

17. Germany lay in ruins after WWI, so a major issue for the "Big Four" victorious powers to settle was how to rebuild Germany.

18. At the Versailles Conference in 1919, Wilson's moral leadership as the American president was enough to assure the adoption of all of his "Fourteen Points."

19. Warren Harding, the leading candidate for the Republican nomination in 1920, was considered one of the most competent members of the Senate.

20. Living quietly in Washington being incapacitated by a stroke and after leaving office, Woodrow Wilson still outlived Warren Harding.

III. Multiple Choice

1. Which of the following was *not* one of the Fourteen Points?

    a. freedom of the seas
    b. reduction of armaments
    c. independence of Poland
    d. freedom of press and spread of information

2. One point of the fourteen came to obsess Wilson more than any other. This was

a. a League of Nations
b. freedom of the seas
c. an end to tariff restraints
d. that Germany should not be punished

3. The man who wanted to strip Germany of territory and saddle the conquered nation with huge reparations payments was

a. Woodrow Wilson
b. Georges Clemenceau
c. Count Nobuaki Makino
d. Secretary of State Robert Lansing

4. Harding sensed that no specific issue was as important to the American people in 1919 as

a. the League of Nations
b. a return to normality
c. a vigorous and active president
d. an end to radicalism

5. Those least likely to get the flu or to die from it if they got it were

a. those growing up in healthy environments
b. farm boys
c. those living in tough, big-city neighborhoods
d. women in childbirth

6. The members of self-appointed guardians of the national interest groups stopped men on the streets to see

a. their draft cards
b. if they supported the war
c. if they had a German accent
d. if they had bought war bonds

7. The Japanese delegates to Versailles were determined to retain for Japan

a. captured German warships
b. food products stored by Germany
c. equal power with western nations
d. the German colonies in the Pacific

8. Which of these is the best example of an organization that successfully responded to the war?

a. Industrial Workers of the World
b. Aircraft Production Board
c. United States Railway Administration
d. the Socialist Party

9. Who won the election of 1920?

a. Herbert Hoover
b. Woodrow Wilson
c. Eugene Debs
d. Warren Harding

10. "Wheatless Mondays" and "Meatless Tuesdays" were examples of

a. voluntary programs organized by Herbert Hoover
b. government rationing of basic food items
c. the Creel Committee's propaganda efforts
d. government coercion, tolerated because of the war

IV. Fill-in Questions

Fill in each blank in the following statements with the correct information.

1. Government spending during the war increased _____, and the executive branch, which had 400,000 employees in 1916, grew to _____ by 1918.

2. The Shipping Board, a federal government agency, produced ships _____ as fast as German U-boats could sink them.

3. The United States Railway Administration changed a 1917 shortage of _____ railroad cars into a surplus of _____ by the end of the war.

4. Chicago reported that housewives had "Hooverized" the garbage down by a _____.

5. Hoover helped increase wheat acreage from 45 million in 1917 to ____ million in 1919.

6. About ____ million young men were inducted through selective service in addition to the _____ million who volunteered.

7. About _____ draftees claimed to be conscientious objectors, although only _____ insisted on being assigned to noncombatant duty.

8. Approximately _____ men refused to cooperate with the military in any way and were imprisoned and treated poorly. The last conscientious objector was not freed from prison until _____.

9. From 2.7 million members in 1914, the union movement grew to _____ million in 1919.

10. The army trained and commissioned more than _____ black officers during the war.

11. Before 1914, only about _____ southern blacks moved north each year; during the war, _____ year left the South for industrial jobs in the North.

12. In 1914, only one _____ of the states had some sort of prohibitionist law on the books, but by 1918 prohibition was the law of the land.

13. The state legislature of New York expelled _____ Socialist assemblymen simply because they objected to the war.

14. The Justice Department raided IWW headquarters in several cities, arrested the union's leadership, and indicted about _____ of them under the Espionage Act of 1917.

15. Overall, _____ German-Americans were imprisoned compared with _____ of Great Britain's much smaller German community.

16. Sauerkraut was renamed "_____" during the war.

17. Nationwide and worldwide, about one _____ of the population caught the Spanish flu, and the death rate was _____ percent.

18. In the congressional elections of 1918, voters returned Republican majorities of _____ to _____ in the House and _____ to _____ in the Senate.

19. Wilson took _____ prominent Republicans with him to the peace conference in Europe.

20. _____ of Wilson's Fourteen Points survived intact at the peace conference.

21. Harding received _____ percent of the vote, more than any candidate who preceded him since popular votes were counted, and the landslide record until 1964.

V. Essay Questions

Write notes under each of the following questions that would help you answer singular essay questions on an exam.

1. Explain the elements of the planned economy. Does this war experience indicate the desirability of a planned economy or is it at best an emergency measure? Explain.

2. What was Hoover's contribution to the war effort? What was meant by "Hooverizing" America? Is there something sinister about the concept of human engineering? Explain.

3. Describe the conditions of blacks during the First World War. Why was the war not effective in ending racism?

4. What was the impact of the war on the lives of women? Was the war responsible for women getting the vote? Explain.

5. Describe the campaign against the Socialists and the I.W.W. Was there any justification for the treatment of these two groups? Why or why not? Should dissent be allowed in wartime? Explain.

6. What were the three efforts by George Creel and the Committee on Public Information? Was this committee and its activities a black mark on United States history? Why or why not?

7. Explain the deception and unrealistic behavior of Woodrow Wilson in 1919 and 1920. To what degree was his stroke the cause of the defeat of the treaty?

8. Describe the peace conference of Versailles and its members. To what extent was this conference the basis for the Second World War?

9. Explain Article 10. Did it commit the United States to go to war if a member of the League of Nations were attacked? Explain.

10. Describe the fight for the League and the result. Was the U.S. defeat of the League a great opportunity lost? Why or why not?

11. Describe the flu epidemic of 1918.

ANSWERS

II. True-False

1. True
2. True
3. True
4. False
5. False
6. False
7. False
8. True
9. False
10. True
11. False
12. False
13. False
14. True
15. True
16. True
17. False
18. False
19. False
20. True

III. Multiple Choice

1. d
2. a
3. b
4. b
5. c
6. a
7. d
8. c
9. d
10. a

IV. Fill-in

1. tenfold; 950,000
2. twice
3. 150,000; 300,000
4. third
5. 75
6. 3; 2
7. 21,000; 4,000
8. 500; 1933
9. 4.2
10. 1,200
11. 10,000; 100,000
12. quarter
13. seven
14. 200
15. 6,300; 45,000
16. "Liberty cabbage"
17. fifth; 3
18. 240; 190; 49; 47
19. no
20. Three
21. 61%

39

The Days of Harding Troubled Years, 1919-1923

"Africa was peopled by a race of cultured black men who were masters in art, science, and literature."

Marcus Garvey

"It is the true office of history to represent the events themselves . . . and to leave the observations and conclusions thereupon to the liberty and faculty of every man's judgment."

Bacon

I. Key Words

You should be able to define the following words and explain their historical significance in relation to the development of American history.

"Roaring Twenties"
Warren G. Harding
"normalcy"
"Babe" Ruth
Herbert Hoover
Charles Evans Hughes
Treaty of Washington
Harry Daugherty
Albert Fall
Teapot Dome
1919 strikes
Boston police strike
Calvin Coolidge
Red Scare
Bolsheviks
Palmer raids
A. Mitchell Palmer
Sacco and Vanzetti case
American Civil Liberties Union
WASPs
William Ripley and Madison Grant
Races of Europe
The Passing of the Great Race

immigration quota system
W.E.B. DuBois
Jim Crow
black nationalism
Marcus Garvey
Universal Negro Improvement Association (UNIA)
Ku Klux Klan
William Simmons
The Birth of a Nation
Eighteenth Amendment
Al Capone
Dearborn Independent
Will Hays
Hays Code
Charles Darwin
fundamentalism
John Scopes
the "Monkey Trial"

II. True-False

If the statement is false, change any words necessary to make it true.

1. Only a small proportion of the American population—the wealthy and the middle class—enjoyed the roaring good times of the twenties.

2. When Harding coined the phrase "normalcy" to describe what the dictionary called "normality," it was because he was barely literate.

3. Despite Harding's personal corruption and administrative ineptitude, his worst fault, according to the text, was his hypocrisy.

4. The Republican Harding pardoned Eugene Debs and other socialists who had opposed American entry into WWI and had been sentenced to federal prison for that crime.

5. By the end of the 1920s, Babe Ruth was paid more than the president of the United States.

6. Not one of Harding's appointments to his cabinet could be called distinguished; most ended up going to jail not long after Harding's death.

7. According to the Treaty of Washington in 1921, Japan, a new naval power, was allowed to have the same size naval fleet as Britain and the United States combined, making Japan the dominant naval power in the Pacific.

8. To comply with the Treaty of Washington, the United States scrapped 30 battleships and cruisers that were planned, under construction, or already in the fleet.

9. The Secretary of the Interior leaded the Navy's petroleum reserves in Wyoming and California to two oilmen in return for a bribe (called a "loan").

10. Never one to waste a resource, Henry Ford invented the charcoal briquette as a way to use wood scraps left over from the manufacture of wooden parts for the Model T.

11. It is now generally concluded that Warren Harding's death came at the hands of his wife, who was well aware of his sexual adventures with other women.

12. It is clear from the anti-strike poster on p. 576 that the steelworkers of 1919 were largely Slavic immigrants rather than the "old-stock" Americans whose ancestors had been in the U.S. for more than a century.

13. When governor Calvin Coolidge ordered the National Guard into Boston to break the police strike, the public disapproved.

14. For years after the end of the European war, "the Hun" continued to be seen as the greatest threat to civilization and humanity.

15. Given that most immigrants were political radicals—socialism was an established European political tradition, and the communist agitators were mostly foreign-born—it probably made good sense to be suspicious of foreigners and to restrict immigration.

16. Madison Grant's book *The Passing of the Great Race* said that the new immigrants were destroying the nation's prized genetic heritage.

17. Lynching finally declined in 1922 after Congress passed, and Coolidge signed, the Dyer Bill.

18. The popularity of black nationalism unnerved whites who were accustomed to a passive black population.

19. At the Democratic National Convention of 1924, the party, despite the Klan, adopted a plan that was critical of bigotry.

20. There was no clear geographical or social dimension to the political battle between "drys" and "wets."

21. The movie industry was founded and dominated by Jews, most of them foreign-born.

22. According to the Hays Code that tried to remove nudity and immorality from the movies, Walt Disney was not allowed to show udders on his cartoon cows.

23. William Jennings Bryan refused to take the stand as an expert witness on the Bible in the "Monkey Trial."

24. Bryan led the prosecution of John Scopes, but collapsed and died in the courtroom before he could finish making his case. Clarence Darrow took over from Bryan and persuaded the jury to convict Scopes on all charges.

III. Multiple Choice

1. If Harding could not hope to be "the best president," he would try to be

   a. in the top ten
   b. the best looking
   c. the best liked
   d. the best dressed

2. Secretary of the Treasury Andrew Mellon pursued tax policies that favored

   a. the rich
   b. the government treasury
   c. the poor
   d. farmers

3. The general strike in Seattle in 1919 was crushed by Mayor Ole Hanson's use of

   a. local lumberjacks, deputized for their willingness to use violence
   b. U.S. Marines
   c. the boycott
   d. deportation of strike leaders

4. The presiding judge in the Sacco and Vanzetti trial was overheard speaking of them as

   a. "basically honest men"
   b. "hard workers"
   c. "probably not guilty"
   d. "damned dagos"

5. Four times Congress failed to pass a bill at would require new immigrants to

   a. have a job before entering the country
   b. pass a literacy test
   c. be of northern European background
   d. submit to a fifteen-year probationary period

6. Marcus Garvey's alternatives to the violent racial conflict was the organization of a powerful

a. union
b. black cultural center in Harlem
c. black nation in Africa
d. militant black "police force"

7. Preachers who demanded that control be slapped on filmmakers, often attributed immorality on the screen to

a. atheists
b. communists
c. the cities and alcohol
d. non-Christian influences

8. The outcome of the "Monkey Trial" was

a. Bryan was found guilty
b. Scopes was found guilty
c. Clarence Darrow won the case
d. Tennessee's law prohibiting the teaching of evolution was overturned

9. Which of these nations was *not* a signer of the Treaty of Washington?

a. Britain
b. United States
c. Japan
d. Germany

10. The "Great Race," according to Madison Grant, was

a. German
b. the new immigrants, whose arrival would increase American diversity
c. limited to paid-up members in the Ku Klux Klan
d. genetically threatened by immigration

IV. Fill-in Questions

Fill each blank in the following statements with the correct information.

1. The modern world's symbol of personal freedom was already in the 1920s the _____.

2. The _____ were the most successful baseball tem in the history of the sport.

3. The 1921 naval arms limitation agreement (Treaty of Washington) set up a ratio of tonnage under which the U.S. and Britain were equal, and Japan's fleet was to be _____ that of the U.S. and Britain.

4. Secretary of the Interior Albert B. Fall leased the navy's petroleum reserves to two oilmen and then accepted loans from the two of about $_____.

5. There were _____ strikes during 1919 involving ____ million workers.

6. Steelworkers worked a ____-hour day and a ____-day week, sometimes ____ hours at a stretch.

7. Attorney Gerald Mitchell's raid on Communist headquarters resulted in the deportation of _____ people, even though only _____ could legally be deported.

8. The Boston police strike of 1919 made _____ a national hero.

9. In April 1919, the Post Office found _____ bombs in the mail addressed to prominent capitalists and government offices.

10. Only _____ of the hundreds of radical Palmer arrested could legally be deported, but he sent _____ on a steamship to Russia.

11. Immigration had declined to _____ in 1918, but soared to _____ in 1921, with most of the immigrants coming from _____ and _____ Europe.

12. In 1921, total annual immigration to the U.S. was limited to _____ people, and each European nation could send a number equal to _____ percent of the number of persons of that nationality already in the U.S. as of _____.

13. In 1924, the immigration law was changed to reduce the total annual immigration to _____, and the annual quota was reduced to _____ percent, and the base year pushed back to _____, before which relatively few immigrants from the "undesirable" countries had arrived.

14. The annual quota after 1924 for Italy was _____, but for Great Britain it was _____, _____ times the number who actually wanted to come.

15. In the Chicago race riot of 1919 _____ people were killed

16. In 1919, _____ blacks were lynched, _____ of them veterans, some still in their military uniforms.

17. Marcus Garvey's UNIA at its peak had over _____ branches in _____ states, mostly in the North.

18. By the mid-1920s membership in the Klan may have been as high as _____ million, but by 1930 had dwindled to _____ members.

19. Between 1906 and 1910, per capita consumption of alcohol in the U.S. was _____ gallons a year; in 1934, consumption stood at _____ gallons. The death rate from chronic alcoholism was _____ per 100,000 in 1907, but just _____ per 100,000 in 1932.

20. Al Capone's bootleg ring grossed $_____ million supplying liquor and beer to Chicagoans during Prohibition.

21. The reason for the Scopes Trial in 1925 was the Tennessee state law that prohibited the teaching of _____ in public schools.

V. Essay Questions

Write notes under each of the following questions that would help you answer essay questions on an exam.

1. What was "roaring" in the "Roaring Twenties"? Is this image of the decade accurate?

2. What were the contradictions of the 1920s?

3. Evaluate Warren G. Harding's presidency. Does he deserve the title "worst president"? Why or why not? Was he responsible for the problems of his administration or was it the aura of the times? Explain.

4. Explain the Treaty of Washington. Could this be considered a first step in disarmament or an example of the futility of the effort to disarm?

5. Describe the strikes and the public reaction to the strikes of 1919 and 1920.

6. What were the reasons for the Red Scare? Why, in a democratic nation that upholds freedom and liberty, would such a development take place?

7. Describe the Sacco and Vanzetti case. If they were actually guilty (at least Sacco), was any harm done by their execution? Explain.

8. Describe the stated reasons for, the methods used, and the outcome of the movement to stop or to slow immigration into the United States in the early 1920s. Was this necessary or was it a betrayal of the American dream? Explain.

9. Describe the Black Scare. Was this worse than the Red Scare? Explain. Was the Black Nationalism movement of Marcus Garvey an answer to racism? Why or why not?

10. What were the characteristics of the Ku Klux Klan in the 1920s? Was the Klan a reasonable response to the threat (or imagined threat) of immigrants, cities, and modern immorality?

10. What were the characteristics of the Ku Klux Klan in the 1920s? Was the Klan a reasonable response to the threat (or imagined threat) of immigrants, cities, and modern immorality?

11. What was the relationship between prohibition and gangsterism? Was this an example of the failure of legislating morality? Why did prohibition not work?

12. Describe the debate over and the trial about teaching evolution. What were the important issues involved? Should a school board that reflects community belief be allowed to forbid the teaching of evolution in public schools? Why? Should a state be allowed to forbid—or to require—particular subjects to be taught? Why?

13. Trace the influence and impact of Protestant fundamentalism on the 1920s, in many diverse areas. Was fundamentalism an effort to restore virtue and a moral society or was it an un-American outbreak of bigotry, and interference in the rights of Americans? Explain.

ANSWERS

II. True-False

1. True
2. False
3. False
4. True
5. True
6. False
7. False
8. True
9. True
10. True
11. False
12. True
13. False
14. False
15. False
16. True
17. False
18. True
19. False
20. False
21. True
22. True
23. False
24. False

III. Multiple Choice

1. c
2. a
3. b
4. d
5. b
6. c
7. d
8. b
9. d
10. d

IV. Fill-in

1. automobile
2. New York Yankees
3. 3/5ths
4. $300,000
5. 3,600; 4
6. 12; seven; 36
7. 249; 39
8. Calvin Coolidge
9. 38
10. 39; 249
11. 110,000; 805,000; southern; eastern
12. 350,000; 3%; 1910
13. 150,000; 2%; 1890
14. 5,802; 75,000; five
15. 38
16. 76; ten
17. 700; 38
18. 4.5; 10,000
19. 2.6; 1.2; 7.3; 2.5
20. $60
21. evolution

40

Calvin Coolidge and the New Era
When America Was Business
1923-1929

"The man who builds a factory builds a temple."
"The business of America is business."

Calvin Coolidge

"Our ignorance of history causes us to slander our own times."

Gustave Flaubert

I. Key Words

You should be able to define the following words and explain their historical significance in relation to the development of American history.

Calvin Coolidge
Herbert Hoover
the New Era
Andrew Mellon
regressive taxation
"trickle down" economic theory
Treaty of Versailles
war debts and the reparations issue
Nan Britton
Kellogg-Briand Pact
tabloid newspapers
Bernarr MacFadden
Al Smith
installment plans
"anxiety advertising"
chain stores
supermarkets
Bruce Barton
The Man Nobody Knows
Florida land boom
speculation
Charles Lindbergh, Jr.

buying on margin"
bull and bear markets
Great Crash of 1929
Great Depression

II. True-False

If the statement is false, change any words necessary to make it true.

1. Calvin Coolidge, like Warren Harding, looked presidential but led a tawdry personal life.

2. Coolidge worshipped financial success and believed without reservation that millionaires knew what was best for the country.

3. Thanks to Coolidge's record of honesty, the Republicans never suffered a voter backlash because of the Harding scandals.

4. The "New Era" of prosperity ended eight months before Coolidge left office, so it is ironic that Herbert Hoover got the blame for the Great Depression.

5. Andrew Mellon sponsored a new federal tax on automobiles.

6. Germany's financial problems in the 1920s were the consequence of reparations demanded by France and Britain after WWI, according to recent research.

7. The Coolidge and Hoover administrations attempted, in a meaningful way, to cooperate with other nations.

8. The Kellogg-Briand Pact of 1928 outlawed war as an instrument of national policy.

9. The United States replaced Great Britain as the chief economic power in Latin America during the 1920s.

10. Herbert Hoover called Prohibition "a great social and economic experiment, noble in motive…"

11. Had Al Smith been a Kansas Presbyterian, who had never even drunk patent medicines, he would have won in 1928.

12. Professional advertisers styled themselves as practical psychologists.

13. A strength of the American economy in the 1920s was the fact that only a few Americans did not share in the good times.

14. Jesus, according to Bruce Barton, would have been an advertising man if he had lived in the 1920s.

15. The Florida land boom of the 1920s was a direct result of the growth of the American population because of immigration and a high birth rate, coupled with a rising standard of living that made oceanfront property desirable.

16. Charles Lindbergh, Jr., chose to fly across the Atlantic in a single-engine light airplane with only himself as the crew, because he was a reckless adventurer by nature (and could not afford a better airplane.)

17. "Buying on margin" meant buying shares only in marginal, or unknown businesses.

18. The value of a share in a corporation theoretically represented the earning capacity of the company.

19. The face value of shares of stock in the Coolidge bull market bore little relationship to the actual health of the American economy, due to speculation.

20. The great stock market crash of 1929 did not cause the Great Depression of the 1930s.

III. Multiple Choice

1. When Dorothy Parker heard Coolidge had died in 1933, she replied,

   a. "Where is the vice-president?"
   b. "There goes a righteous man."
   c. "How could they tell?"
   d. "He would have avoided the depression."

2. Mellon paid for the cost of government through tariffs and an increase of kinds of taxes paid by the

   a. middle and lower classes
   b. rich
   c. corporations
   d. farmers

3. Mellon believed that businessmen reinvested their profits, which then would

   a. bring more profits
   b. "trickle down" to the middle and lower classes
   c. give them more prestige with the public
   d. create fewer jobs

4. Experts warned that to continue to bleed Germany for reparations payments would promote

a. a Russian invasion
b. peace in central Europe
c. economies of France and England
d. political extremism in Germany

5. Which of these Latin American nations was occupied by U.S. Marines for at least some part of the 1920s?

a. Nicaragua
b. Cuba
c. Haiti
d. all of these

6. Down to 1920, Americans borrowed money to invest in ways that would increase their income, but in the 1920s Americans began to borrow in order to

a. live more comfortably
b. pay their debts
c. buy stocks and bonds
d. establish credit

7. Underarm deodorants, without which humanity had functioned for millennia, were made necessary in the 1920s by

a. new social relationships
b. diet changes
c. anxiety advertising
d. the odor from gasoline engines

8. Andrew Mellon's tax policies included all but which of these?

a. higher taxes on the rich
b. a tax on automobiles
c. an increase in regressive taxes
d. a high tariff

9. Who was "The Man Nobody Knows," in the book of the same name?

a. Calvin Coolidge
b. Charles Lindbergh
c. Bruce Barton
d. Jesus

10. "Buying on margin" meant

a. borrowing up to 90% of the cost of a share of stock
b. using the anticipated higher future value of stocks as collateral
c. disaster, if the stock market went down instead of up
d. all of these

IV. Fill-in Questions

Fill in each blank in the following statements with the correct information.

1. Alice Roosevelt Longworth said Calvin Coolidge looked as if he had been weaned on a _____.

2. Coolidge's idea of a good time was a _____; according to the text, he spent at least _____ hours a day in bed.

3. Though he was nicknamed "_____," Coolidge gave _____ speeches in 1925, when nothing much happened, compared to the _____ that Woodrow Wilson gave in 1917, the year the U.S. went to war.

4. Andrew Mellon reduced personal income tax for people who made more than $_____ a year and refunded $_____ million to United States Steel.

5. Nan Britton's account of her affair with Warren Harding, *The President's Daughter,* sold _____ copies in 1927.

6. Eventually, _____ nations signed the Kellogg-Briand Pact, including the nations that would soon violate its intent.

7. American investments in Latin America climbed from about $_____ million in 1914 to $_____ billion in 1929.

8. By 1924, American officials directly or indirectly administered the finances of _____ Latin American countries.

9. Herbert Hoover won ____ percent of the popular vote in 1928.

10. Between 1920 and 1929, wages increased by an average of ____ percent, but stock dividends rose ____ percent.

11. As a result of the widespread acceptance of installment buying, ____ percent of all automobiles were bought on time, and ____ percent of washing machines.

12. The growth of the supermarket is illustrated by the growth of the A&P chain, which grew from _____ to _____ stores between 1920 and 1929.

13. Standard Oil owned ____ gas stations in 1920; by 1929 it owned _____.

14. Henry Ford's income was $_____ a day for most of the 1920s

15. Some lots in Miami Beach changed hands a _____ times within a few months, and a Miami newspaper had more than _____ pages of advertisements of land for sale.

16. "Buying on margin" meant paying as little as ____ percent of the price of a share of stock, borrowing the rest from a broker (who in turn borrowed the money from banks whose depositors usually had no idea their uninsured savings were fueling speculation in the stock market.)

17. Over ____ million Americans were "playing the market" in 1926.

18. During the 1920s, women owned _____ percent of the nation's wealth and made _____ percent of all stock market transactions.

19. On "Black Thursday," October 24th, 1919, a record _____ million shares changed hands, and values collapsed. The following Tuesday, speculators dumped _____ million shares.

20. When the dust settled early in the morning of October 30, 1929, more than $_____ billion in paper value of stocks had been wiped out.

V. Essay Questions

Write notes under each of the following questions that would help you answer similar essay questions on an exam.

1. Explain Secretary of Treasurer Mellon's tax policies. What evidence is there for his philosophical approach that capitalists would reinvest their tax savings and that the profits would "trickle down" to the middle and lower classes?

2. What were the problems involved in reparations and the war debt? Who was right and who was wrong in the dilemma? What would have been the best solution? Explain.

3. Was United States involvement in Latin America in the 1920s a case of businessmen putting their profits over the national interest? Explain.

4. Describe the election of 1928. Were the "hidden issues" of religion and location (city and country) more important than substantial issues of economy and foreign policy? Explain.

5. Explain the impact of consumer credit and advertising on the American economy. Did the U.S. economy make a wrong turn when it allowed people to buy on credit and advertisers to create new needs? Why or why not?

6. Why did chain stores come into existence? Was this a positive development in retailing? What benefits resulted to the consumer? What were some unintended consequences?

7. Describe the business culture of the 1920s. Why would *The Man Nobody Knows* become a best-selling book in the 1920s?

8. Describe the process of playing the stock market and the consequences in 1929. Should something have been done by the President, economists, brokers, or corporations to restrain the speculation mania? Why or why not?

9. What is meant by the sentence, "The Great Crash of 1929 did not cause the Great Depression of the 1930s?" Has the Great Crash been given too much publicity and clouded out the underlying weaknesses in the economy of the 1920s? Explain.

10. Describe the flight of Charles Lindbergh across the Atlantic. Is he a true hero or just a product of luck and coincidence? Explain.

ANSWERS

II. True-False

1. False
2. True
3. True
4. False
5. True
6. False
7. False
8. True
9. True
10. True
11. False
12. True
13. False
14. True
15. False
16. False
17. False
18. True
19. True
20. True

III. Multiple Choice

1. c
2. a
3. b
4. d
5. d
6. a
7. c
8. a
9. d
10. d

IV. Fill-in

1. pickle
2. nap; 12
3. "Silent Cal"; 28; 17
4. $60,000; $15
5. 50,000
6. 62
7. $800; $5.4

8. 10
9. 58%
10. 24%; 65%
11. 60%; 90%
12. 4,621; 15,418
13. 12; 1,000
14. $25,000
15. dozen; 500
16. 10%
17. 1.5
18. 40%; 35%
19. 13; 16
20. $30

41

National Trauma
The Great Depression
1930-1933

"A chicken in every pot and two cars in every garage."
"You went a-fishing, let the country go to ruin"

"I hold the view that the greatest changes in human history are to be traced back to internal caused conditions, and that they are founded upon internal psychological necessity."

C. G. Jung

I.   Key Words

You should be able to define the following words and explain their historical significance in relation to the development of American history.

Great Depression
unemployment rate
soup kitchens and bread lines
Hoovervilles
"Okies" and "Arkies"
Reconstruction Finance Corporation (RFC)
"trickle-down" economics
"rugged individualism"
Norman Thomas
National Farmers' Holiday Association
Bonus March of 1932; "Bonus Boys"
Douglas MacArthur
1930s gangsters; "Bonnie and Clyde"
Shirley Temple
Busby Berkeley
"New Deal"
Amos 'n' Andy
"brains trust"

II. True-False

If the statement is false, change any words necessary to make it true.

1. The depression generation was the last American generation to date whose character and values were forged in an era of drastic economic decline and deprivation.

2. The Great Depression brought political liberals into power, but by the 1950s, voters had forgotten the hardships of the 1930s and repudiated most New Deal policies.

3. The stock market crashed in 1929, but had recovered most of the losses of the crash by 1932.

4. Most of the hardships suffered as a result of the Great Crash were endured by the very rich, to judge by the general lack of interest the public had for soup kitchens and similar charitable efforts.

5. "Okies" and "Arkies" were refugees from dust storms and rural poverty who thought they could improve their lives by going to California.

6. One of the underlying causes of the Great Depression was a shortage of food, because so many farmers had given up farming and moved to the city during the 1930s.

7. "Hoovervilles" were special housing for the poor, paid for by President Hoover himself.

8. Hoover broke with the Coolidge-Mellon policies of withdrawing the federal government from active intervention in the economy.

9. The RFC was a popular program of relief for big businesses that would eventually reach the working man.

10. Boulder Dam, later renamed Hoover Dam, was the first great public works program of the Great Depression.

11. Hoover insisted that the government must spend no more money than it collected; the books must balance.

12. What was particularly puzzling to Hoover and his advisors was that the economic problems of the United States by 1932 were unique—no other industrialized nation was having a depression.

13. The radio program "Amos 'n' Andy" (with its lead characters played by two white men speaking in southern black dialect) was so offensive to African Americans that it was taken off the air after less than a year.

14. The board game Monopoly was introduced during the Great Depression and sold millions of sets.

15. Most Americans interpreted the Great Depression as evidence that capitalism had failed.

16. For the most part, Americans coped with the depression peacefully and without a thought for revolution.

17. The Communists were the most influential organization among the Bonus Boys.

18. Most labor unions in the 1930s were dominated by Communists, and many American workers converted to an anticapitalist ideology as they saw firsthand the failure of the economic system based on the private ownership of property.

19. Thoroughly discredited by the events of the Depression, Herbert Hoover still tried to run for reelection in 1932, but his own Republican party would not nominate him.

20. Franklin Roosevelt won the election of 1932 because he spelled out in precise detail exactly the kind of new government programs his "New Deal" would create.

III.   Multiple Choice

1. Hundreds of thousands of people lost their homes between 1929 and 1933 because they could not

   a. pay taxes
   b. keep families together
   c. meet mortgage payments
   d. afford maintenance and repairs

2. Because so many people hitched rides on freight trains, railroads decided to

   a. shoot to kill
   b. give up keeping people off
   c. remove all ladders from freight cars
   d. employ Pinkerton detectives to keep them off

3. One of the signs of poverty in the depression was a pocket turned inside-out, which was called

   a. a Hoover flag
   b. empty treasury
   c. "that's all folks"
   d. showing the truth

4. The most conspicuous consequence of the water conservation and power generation of the Hoover Dam was

a. to bring praise and recognition to Hoover
b. to irrigate the Great Plains throughout the West
c. to create scarcity of water in California
d. to make Las Vegas a gambling center

5. Hoover was a self-made man and had forgotten that to get ahead he needed

a. money
b. good luck
c. friends
d. a depression

6. Hoover viewed government as a

a. football game
b. Stanford faculty association
c. business
d. an engineering project

7. During the depression, sociologists and journalists reported on interviews with homeless hitchhikers who

a. complained about the capitalist system
b. wondered if the Soviet system was better
c. pleaded for jobs
d. apologized for their shabby clothing

8. At the worst point in the Great Depression, the national unemployment rate was

a. 25%
b. 50%
c. 80%
d. almost 100% among African American workers

9. Which of these illustrates the personal popularity of the American president in 1932?

a. Hoovervilles
b. Hoover blankets
c. Hoover Pullmans
d. none of these

10. According to the text, the "depression-proof" industry was

a. automobiles
b. agriculture
c. movies
d. railroads

IV. Fill-in Questions

Fill in each blank in the following statements with the correct information.

1. During the first year after the crash of the stock market, ____ million Americans lost their jobs. By 1931, _____ people were being fired each week.

2. By 1932, _____ percent of the workforce was unemployed. A year later; one farm family in _____ was pushed off the land.

3. Between 1929 and 1933, the average weekly earnings of manufacturing workers fell from $_____ to less than $_____.

4. The wholesale price of cotton fell to ____ cents a pound, and corn growers who could not sell their harvest were _____ it.

5. When a Soviet agency announced openings for skilled technicians who were willing to move to Russia, _____ Americans said they would go.

6. More than _____ small businesses went bankrupt from 1929 to 1933, _____ just in 1932.

7. When the city government of Birmingham called for 800 workers to put in an ____-hour day for $_____, _____ applicants showed up.

8. Philadelphia's social workers managed to reach only one _____ of the city's unemployed in order to provide $_____ in relief to a family for a week.

9. Statistics gathered by the Missouri Pacific Railroad counted _____ people hopping its freight trains in 1928, but _____ three years later.

10. The birth rate declined from 3 million in 1921 to ____ million in 1932.

11. Will Rogers quipped that the United States would be the first country to go to the poorhouse in an _____.

12. Hoover spent $_____ a year on public works in an effort to create jobs.

13. Socialist party presidential candidate Norman Thomas won _____ votes in the 1928 election, but _____ in 1932.

14. The "last nail in Hoover's coffin" was the Army's attack on the _____ camp in Washington.

15. Admission to the movies was typically _____ cents for adults, and _____ cents for children.

16. Shirley Temple's annual salary was $_____ and her films made $_____ million a year for Fox Pictures.

17. A 78-rpm record sold for _____ cents, but a radio could be bought for $_____ or $_____ and operated for the cost of electricity.

18. Roosevelt's campaign song (and that of the Democratic party ever since) was "_____."

19. Roosevelt received _____ electoral votes in 1932 to Hoover's _____.

20. The appearance of the "brains trust" indicated that, though the nation's capital was a businessman's town in the 1920s, the people who would be running the country in the 1930s would be _____.

V. Essay Questions

Write notes under each of the following questions that would help you answer similar essay questions on an exam.

1. Describe the depression in numerical and statistical terms. Which gives a better picture of the depression—the numbers or anecdotes of tragedy? Why?

2. What was the approach, attitude, and action of Hoover in dealing with the depression? Could he have been expected to do more? Explain. Was Hoover a case of someone caught between principles and reality? Explain.

3. Explain the philosophy of Herbert Hoover regarding the American spirit and the business cycle.

4. Describe the Marxist and Socialist efforts in the 1930s. Why did these groups fail, even though they proposed solutions to the crisis?

5. What was the attitude of the American people toward capitalism in the midst of the depression? How can this attitude be explained?

6. To what extent was the Bonus Boys' dispersion a sign of Hoover's lack of sympathy and understanding? What would a more humanitarian response have been?

7. Describe the activities of "Robin Hood" gangsters of the depression. Does the public admiration for them indicate that something was wrong with the legitimate system? Why or why not?

8. What were the beneficial contributions of the movies and music to the gloomy conditions during the depression? Did film and music possibly help avoid more serious violent outbreaks during the 1930s? Explain your answer.

9. Describe the election of 1932. Is there any possible way a Republican candidate could have won the 1932 election? What was FDR's program? How specific was he in describing it?

10. What was the impact of the radio on American life? Explain the controversy over the "Amos 'n' Andy" show in the 1960s.

ANSWERS

II. True-False

1. True
2. False
3. False
4. False
5. True
6. False
7. False
8. True
9. False
10. True
11. True
12. False
13. False
14. True
15. False
16. True
17. False
18. False
19. False
20. False

III. Multiple Choice

1. c
2. b
3. a
4. d
5. b
6. c
7. d
8. a
9. d
10. c

IV. Fill-in

1. 4; 100,000
2. 25%; four
3. $25; $17
4. 5 cents; burning
5. 100,000
6. 100,000; 32,000
7. 11; $2; 12,000
8. fifth; $4.23
9. 14,000; 186,000
10. 2.4
11. automobile
12. $500
13. 267,000; 882,000
14. Bonus Boys'
15. 25 cents; 10 cents
16. $300,000; 5
17. 35 cents; $10; $20
18. "Happy Days Are Here Again"
19. 472; 59
20. intellectuals

42

Rearranging America
FDR and the New Deal, 1933-1938

"The President wants you to join the union."

"It is common sense to take a method and try it. If it fails, admit it frankly and try another."

Franklin D. Roosevelt

"All that historians give us are little oases in the desert of time, and we linger fondly in these, forgetting the vast tracks between one and another that were troubled by the weary generations of man."

J. A. Spender

I. Key Words

You should be able to define the following words and explain their historical significance in relation to the development of American history.

Franklin Delano Roosevelt
"fireside chats"
bank holiday
"brains trust"
Eleanor Roosevelt
the Hundred Days
Emergency Banking Act
Federal Emergency Relief Administration (FERA)
John Maynard Keynes
"Keynesian" economics
Civilian Conservation Corps (CCC)
Civil Works Administration (CWA)
Works Progress Administration (WPA)
Twenty-first Amendment
National Recovery Administration (NRA)
Section 7(a) of the NIRA
"We Do Our Part" and the Blue Eagle
National Labor Relations Act (NLRA) or Wagner Act

National Labor Relations Board (NLRB)
Agricultural Adjustment Administration (AAA)
parity (in agriculture)
Rural Electrification Administration (REA)
Tennessee Valley Authority (TVA)
George Norris
Muscle Shoals
American Liberty League
Charles Coughlin
Francis Townsend
Huey Long ("The Kingfish")
Social Security Act of 1935
Mary McLeod Bethune
Oscar De Priest
John L. Lewis
Committee on Industrial Organization/Congress of Industrial Organizations (CIO)
American Federation of Labor
United Steel Workers
United Automobile Workers
"Memorial Day Massacre"
"Bloody Harlan"

II. True-False

If the statement is false, change any words necessary to make it true.

1. Woodrow Wilson's wife, Edith Galt Wilson, Henry Cabot Lodge, and the political columnist Walter Lippmann all dismissed Franklin Roosevelt as a pleasant and charming man who was essentially unqualified to become president.

2. FDR's family was an old New York family that had once been wealthy, but in recent years had fallen on hard times.

3. FDR married a distant cousin, Eleanor; another distant cousin was Theodore Roosevelt.

4. Shortly after taking office, FDR ordered the nation's banks to close, using emergency presidential powers.

5. Despite the doubts of many of his critics, historians now agree that Roosevelt's greatest strength was what Supreme Court Justice Oliver Wendell Holmes called his "first-class intellect."

6. One of the handicaps of Roosevelt was an outspoken wife who often took stands and made statements that were politically unwise.

7. During the Hundred Days, Roosevelt and his brain trusters were virtually unopposed; FDR's proposals sailed through Congress without serious debate.

8. In April, 1933, FDR took the nation off the gold standard; paper money could no longer be exchanged for gold, and gold could not be exported.

9. Harry Hopkins, director of the Federal Emergency Relief Administration (FERA) disliked handouts, and wanted able-bodied recipients of government relief to work in return for their assistance.

10. The Civilian Conservation Corps was one of the least popular government programs, because it was run by the U.S. Army, but it put nearly three million young men to work.

11. The Works Progress Administration (WPA) built public buildings, as had been true of the earlier Civil Works Administration (CWA), but it also hired people to paint pictures, write plays and books, and do a large oral history project on slavery.

12. An Appalachian song praising Roosevelt pointed to repeal of the income tax as his most important act.

13. Industrial codes written by the NRA even extended to peripheral and trivial businesses—even to burlesque shows, but the entire program was ruled unconstitutional.

14. The one part of the National Industrial Recovery Act that survived the demise of the NRA was the provision requiring that employers recognize and bargain with labor unions, if a majority of a company's employees supported a union.

15. The New Deal's farm program had an unfortunate side effect—by requiring farmers to plant fewer acres, it caused landowners to throw tenants and sharecroppers off the land. Commodity prices, however, did rise.

16. FDR's Tennessee Valley Authority was actually the idea of a Republican senator from Nebraska, who had to fight off Henry Ford to keep the first site of the project in government hands.

17. In an effort to keep the old radical novelist, Upton Sinclair, from being elected as the Democratic governor of California in 1934, the Republicans spent a million dollars more than they had spent on Herbert Hoover's national campaign in 1932.

18. Huey Long of Louisiana was a typical southern race-baiting politician who, once elected, provided state services only to white voters.

19. FDR's many powerful political enemies, combined with voter resentment at the continuation of economic problems, made the 1936 election a close race.

20. Most of the violence in the U.S. in the 1930s was related to union organization, and most of it was caused by employers or the police.

21. Historians now agree that the New Deal ended the Great Depression.

22. The New Deal ushered in an age of socialism, since the federal government took over so many of the nation's basic industries.

23. The success of the New Deal made the Democrats the nation's majority political party.

24. Another legacy of the New Deal was a greatly expanded federal government bureaucracy.

25. FDR's reform of the federal income tax confiscated 100% of all income in excess of $1 million a year, effectively abolishing the wealthiest class in America.

III. Multiple Choice

1. In the end Roosevelt's great strength was his

   a. birth and background
   b. bout with polio
   c. flexibility
   d. good looks

2. Whereas F. D. R. was a cool, detached, and calculating politician whom few got to know well, Eleanor was

   a. aloof and unconcerned
   b. compassionate and moved by injustice
   c. philosophical, a woman of principle
   d. rather light-headed

3. The Emergency Banking Act eliminated weak banks merely by

   a. identifying them
   b. making them illegal
   c. severely regulating them
   d. ignoring them

4. One of the New Deal's most popular programs was the

   a. Relief Administration
   b. Home Owners' Loan Association
   c. aid to farmers
   d. Civilian Conservation Corps

5. Under the NRA codes, a business was bound by its industry's code not by moral suasion but

a. by example of others in the industry
b. by force of law
c. by Roosevelt's edict
d. the threat of heavier taxes

6. The new Democratic majority consisted of all but which of these voting blocs?

a. southern whites
b. blue-collar workers, particularly union members
c. African Americans
d. members of the Liberty League

7. The National Labor Relations Act of 1935 guaranteed the right of unions to represent workers who

a. voted for a union in NLRB supervised elections
b. did not advocate strikers
c. were skilled and not easily replaced
d. were not Communists

8. Which of these New Deal agencies collected oral histories of former slaves?

a. CCC
b. CWA
c. WPA
d. NRA

9. FDR's main interest in the New Deal was

a. to save the people and the nation
b. to shift control of the economy to the government
c. to balance the federal budget at almost all costs
d. establish a welfare system and promote socialism

10. The New Deal's farm policy intended to

a. force sharecroppers and tenants off the land
b. raise farm prices by restricting production
c. increase farm production to feed the starving unemployed
d. lower the cost of food by cutting the income farmers received

IV. Fill-in Questions

Fill in each blank in the following statements with the correct information.

1. Franklin Roosevelt was descended from or related by marriage to _____ presidents of the United States who had preceded him.

2. FDR held _____ press conferences in 1933 and _____ in 1940; recent presidents have held no more than four or five a year.

3. FDR's order that all the nation's banks would be closed temporarily was called a _____.

4. FDR's one most indispensable aide was _____.

5. In April 1933, the United States went off the gold standard, and the price of gold was frozen by law at $_____ an ounce.

6. Roosevelt established the FERA, which distributed $_____ million to states for relief programs.

7. The British economics John Maynard Keynes (whose ideas FDR didn't understand, but followed somewhat anyway) argues that _____ and not _____ was the key to prosperity in a modern industrial economy, and to stimulate the economy, the federal government should spend money it did not have.

8. The CCC employed _____ million young men earning $_____ a month to work in conservation projects.

9. The WPA from 1935 to 1943 spent more than $_____ billion and employed _____ million people.

10. The National Youth Administration provided jobs for _____ million high school and college students.

11. Fully a _____ of the 1933 cotton crop was plowed under, and within two years cotton prices rose by over _____ percent.

12. Between 1932 and 1935, in part because of the New Deal's farm program (but also due to economic conditions and the continuing mechanization of agriculture), _____ million American farmers were forced off the land.

13. Dr. Francis E. Townsend proposed a monthly pension of $_____ to all people over 60 years old if they did not work and spent it all within the month.

14. Voters in Maine liked to claim that their voters tended to pick the winner in most presidential elections, under the slogan "As Maine goes, so goes the _____." FDR's campaign manager, James Farley, predicted the actual outcome of the Electoral College vote in 1936 when he said, "As goes Maine, so goes _____."

15. Blacks shared in the relief programs, and blacks moved into more than a _____ of the new housing units constructed by the federal government.

16. In 1932, about _____ percent of American black voters were Republicans, but by 1936, _____ percent of registered blacks were voting Democratic, and the only black Republican congressman, _____, was defeated by a Democrat.

17. When Roosevelt took office in 1933, union membership was less than _____ million, but by 1941, union membership was at more than _____ million.

18. The number of federal employees rose from _____ in 1930 to _____ million in 1940.

19. Government spending in preparation for _____ finally ended the Great Depression

20. Between 1930 and 1997, the Republicans simultaneously controlled the presidency, the Senate and the House just _____ years, and to date there have never been more than ____ Republican Senators out of 100.

V. Essay Questions

Write notes under each of the following questions that would help you answer similar essay questions on an exam.

1. Describe Franklin Roosevelt's strengths and weaknesses. Was he the "man for the times"? A recent president has said that the United States "went wrong" beginning in 1932. What evidence is there for such a view?

2. What were Eleanor Roosevelt's contributions to the presidency? Was it proper for the unelected wife of a president to be so active? Why or why not?

3. List and explain briefly the New Deal programs from 1933 to 1935.

4. What was the New Deal solution to farmer's problems? What did the AAA try to do, and what were some unintended consequences of New Deal farm policy?

5. Describe the TVA program. Was the organization of the TVA typical of most New Deal programs?

6. Describe the beliefs of the three main rivals to Roosevelt in the 1930s—Long, Coughlin, and Townsend. Who was most dangerous to Roosevelt? Why? Why did none succeed?

7. What was the New Deal attitude toward blacks? In what ways was black progress encouraged even though programs were not designed for them?

8. Describe the growth of labor unions during the New Deal. Why were some companies so much opposed to unions? Why was there such a growth in union activity only after 1935?

9. Evaluate the results of the New Deal. Did the New Deal save capitalism, or did it usher in an age of socialism?

10. What was the political revolution connected with the New Deal?

ANSWERS

II. True-False

1. True
2. False
3. True
4. True
5. False
6. False
7. True
8. True
9. True
10. False
11. True
12. False
13. True
14. True
15. True
16. True
17. True
18. False
19. False
20. True
21. False
22. False
23. True
24. True
25. False

III. Multiple Choice

1. c
2. b
3. a
4. d
5. b
6. d
7. a
8. c
9. a
10. b

IV. Fill-in

1. 11
2. 83; 96
3. bank holiday
4. Eleanor Roosevelt
5. $35
6. $500
7. consumption; investment
8. 2.9; $30
9. $11; 8.5
10. 2
11. quarter; 50%
12. 3
13. $300
14. nation; Vermont
15. third
16. 75%; 75%; Oscar De Priest
17. 3; 10.5
18. 600,000; 1
19. war (WWII)
20. two; 55

43

Another Great War
America and the World
1933-1942

"Freedom of speech and expression, freedom of worship, freedom from want, freedom from fear."

"I'll Be Seeing You"

"Greetings"

"I have always been convinced that individual and collective crimes are closely linked; and in my capacity of journalist I have only tried to make clear that the day to day horrors of our political history are no more than the visible consequences of the invisible history unfolding in the secrecy of the human heart."

Francis Mauriac

I. Key Words

You should be able to define the following words and explain their historical significance in relation to the development of American history.

Cordell Hull
Henry Stimson
Good Neighbor Policy
Platt Amendment
Chiang Kai-shek
Stimson Doctrine
Soviet Union
Joseph Stalin
Gerald Nye
"merchants of death"
Neutrality Acts
Anschluss
"Third Reich"
Sudetenland
Benito Mussolini
Adolph Hitler

Mein Kampf
Hirohito
"phony war"
Maginot Line
Blitzkrieg
Dunkirk evacuation
Rome-Berlin Axis
"cash-and-carry" policy
Burke-Wadsworth Act
Wendell Willkie
Lend-Lease
"wolf packs"
Atlantic Charter
USS *Reuben James*
Office of Price Administration (OPA)
rationing and scrap drives
"victory gardens"
America First Committee
Open Door Policy
Pearl Harbor
Isoroku Yamamoto
Jeannette Rankin
"Gold Star" mothers
"dollar-a-year men"
National War Labor Board
Office of War Mobilization
Henry J. Kaiser
Liberty Ships
Women's Airforce Service Pilots (WASP)
Tuskegee Airmen
"Rosie the Riveter"

II. True-False

If the statement is false, change any words necessary to make it true.

1. Roosevelt passed over diplomats in naming his Secretary of State and made a political appointment, Cordell Hull.

2. The "Good Neighbor" policy was a Hoover idea that FDR adopted.

3. During WWII, Nazi Germany was able to exploit anti-Americanism in Latin America and establish several critical U-boat and air bases in the Western Hemisphere.

4. Roosevelt's diplomatic recognition of the Soviet Union (which previous presidents had refused to grant) came primarily because of his communist sympathies.

5. By 1935 most Americans believed that the United States had vital interests to protect in Europe and Asia.

6. In 1935, Italy invaded Ethiopia, one of only two independent nations in Africa.

7. In March 1939, Hitler seized all of Czechoslovakia, whose people were German in language and culture.

8. Japan was a modern industrial nation that was poor in the basic natural resources needed for industrial power.

9. The Italian word "duce" and the German word "Führer" mean the same thing—"leader."

10. Instead of invading Great Britain with a land force, Hitler ordered relentless aerial bombardment of the country.

11. Hitler's greatest mistake was to postpone, then cancel his planned invasion of Britain.

12. The fall of France and the heroic resistance of Britain did not change American attitudes towards neutrality.

13. Wendell Willkie, the Republican candidate in 1940, did not disagree with Roosevelt on any essentials.

14. The Lend-Lease Act of 1941 made the United States the "arsenal of democracy" for the Allied war effort.

15. The first ship sunk at Pearl Harbor was an old American destroyer, the USS *Reuben James*.

16. Japanese planes sank two of the three American aircraft carriers at Pearl Harbor.

17. Japanese war aims in China could not be reconciled with America's Open Door policy.

18. Admiral Yamamoto, the Japanese planner of the Pearl Harbor surprise attack, opposed war with the United States and predicted disaster for Japan if a war lasted more than six months to a year.

19. Jeannette Rankin, a Montana pacifist, was the only vote against a U.S. declaration of war on Japan after Pearl Harbor. She had also voted against U.S. entry into WWI..

20. According to the text, FDR knew where and when the Japanese attack was going to be made, but deliberately failed to inform the Army or the Navy, because he wanted the U.S. to enter the war.

21. So convinced were Americans of the rightness of their cause that more enlisted than had to be drafted into military service.

22. Sewell Avery, who resisted government authority during WWII and was carried bodily off to jail, was typical of most big businessmen during the war.

23. Blacks won a sense of security, which had been unknown to earlier generations, because of the generally antiracist policies of the young CIO unions.

24. "Rosie the Riveter" was the first modern example of the American feminist movement.

25. There was a kind of good-humored innocence about the way Americans fought the Second World War.

III. Multiple Choice

1. In November 1933, Roosevelt formally recognized

a. Mexico
b. the Soviet government
c. the threat of Hitler
d. the Stimson Doctrine

2. Critics of the Neutrality Acts argued that they worked to the disadvantage of countries that

a. were innocent victims of aggression
b. needed more trade
c. were south of the equator
d. practiced imperialism

3. Hitler knew what the wanted and said so in his autobiography:

a. a German place in the world
b. German-speaking people to be unified in Germany
c. a socialist society
d. German domination of Europe

4. During the winter of 1939/1940, journalists spoke of a "phony war" in which

a. both sides negotiated for peace
b. spies were sent to many nations
c. neither side attacked the other with force
d. Hitler merely wanted to frighten France

5. The American Communist party in the autumn of 1942 joined

a. the pro-war camp
b. the "save China" program
c. the antiwar activists
d. the Soviet International

6. The America First Committee's case was weakened because most of its members agreed that the United States

a. should declare war
b. should arm for defense
c. adopt pacifism
d. should not arm and antagonize Hitler

7. The most important agency in the war was the

a. War Labor Board
b. Office of Price Administration
c. Federal Reserve Board
d. Office of War Mobilization

8. The Good Neighbor policy was directed at

a. the Soviet Union
b. China and Japan
c. Central and South America
d. Germany

9. The Neutrality Acts passed between 1935 and 1937

a. required belligerent nations to pay cash for weapons bought in the U.S.
b. allowed belligerent nations to borrow money from American banks
c. warned Americans not to travel on ships flying the flags of warring nations
d. revoked American membership in the League of Nations

10. The first American warship sunk as a result of enemy action was

a. the USS *Arizona*
b. the USS *Reuben James*
c. the USS *Prince of Wales*
d. the USS *Liberty*

IV. Fill-in Questions

Fill in each blank in the following statements with the correct information.

1. Secretary of State Hull negotiated reciprocal trade agreements with _____ countries.

2. According to one public opinion poll taken in 1935, ____ percent of Americans were isolationists, believing that the United States had _____ vital interests to protect in either Europe or Asia.

3. "Merchants of death" were _____ makers, according to Senator _____ of South Dakota.

4. Japan was America's _____ largest customer, importing cotton, copper, _____ and _____.

5. Hitler's government first stripped of Jews of their _____ and then murdered them in extermination camps.

6. The German word *Blitzkrieg* meant literally "_____."

7. The German invasion of the Soviet Union put _____ million Soviet troops out of commission by late 1941; Hitler lost _____ men in the first year of the Russian war.

8. Between March 1940 and July, the percentage of Americans who thought that a Germany victory in Europe would threaten the U.S. changed from _____ percent to almost ____ percent.

9. Restrictions on driving (including a national speed limit of _____ miles per hour) were imposed in order to save _____.

10. In 1943, despite rationing, the American standard of living was _____ percent higher than it had been in 1939.

11. When WWII began, the U.S. was spending $_____ billion a month on the military, but during the first half of 1942, the expenditure rose to $_____ billion monthly. By its end, the cost of WWII came to more than $_____ billion.

12. General Motors received _____ percent of all federal expenditures between 1941 and 1945.

13. FDR announced in 1942 that "Dr. New Deal" had been replaced by "Dr. _____."

14. About _____ Liberty ships were built between 1941 and 1944.

15. The size of the federal government swelled from _____ million civilian employees in 1940 to _____ million in 1945, and state government grew at the same rate.

16. In 1944 alone, American factories built _____ airplanes (_____ a day).

17. By 1943 Henry J. Kaiser's Liberty ships were being christened at the rate of ____ each day.

18. California's population grew from _____ million in 1940 to _____ million in 1950, thanks to the growth of West Coast defense industries.

19. Real wages rose _____ percent during the war.

20. By the time the fighting was over, _____ Americans were dead.

V. Essay Questions

Write notes under each of the following questions that would help you answer similar essay questions on an exam.

1. Describe Roosevelt's application of the Good Neighbor Policy. In the long run was this policy better than a policy of intervention? Explain.

2. Explain the Stimson Doctrine. Why would economic sanctions not be applied against Japan? Should a more forceful action have been taken by the United States? Why or why not?

3. What were the arguments of the isolationists? Were Senator Nye's charges true and important? Why?

4. Describe the neutrality legislation of the 1930s. What did the Neutrality Acts prohibit, and why?

5. What were the preliminaries that led to World War II? How and at what points might these actions have been curtailed or avoided?

6. What were the reasons for the aggressor nations' aggression? Could their demands have been satisfied without war or was war inevitable given their attitudes? Explain.

7. Describe the nationalist, patriotic viewpoints of Japan, Italy, and Germany. Are all nations subject to developments in this direction or only those cited above? Explain.

8. Describe the first two years of the war. Was the invasion of the USSR was a grave mistake by Hitler? Explain.

9. What were Roosevelt's steps short of war? Did he, by these steps, bring us into the war?

10. List and explain the steps that led the United States into war with Japan. Who was responsible for the disaster at Pearl Harbor? Do you agree that the reason for the Pearl Harbor disaster was "the chronic incompetence in all large organizations"? Explain.

11. Describe the organizing success of the United States in fighting the Second World War. In what ways did the New Deal prepare the nation for this success?

12. Describe rationing during World War II. Were rationing and scrap drives more important as psychological ploys to rally support for the war than actual ways of saving vital materials? Explain.

VII. Chronology

Number the following events in their correct chronological order from 1 to 15.

a. The "Phony War" in Europe
b. Hitler forces the political union of Austria and Germany
c. Japanese attack Pearl Harbor
d. First of the Neutrality Acts becomes law
e. Hitler's army invades the Soviet Union
f. Germany's invasion of Poland starts World War II in Europe
g. Roosevelt runs for a third term
h. Stimson Doctrine (nonrecognition of aggression)
i. France collapses to German forces
j. The United States formally recognizes the Soviet Union
k. Sinking of the USS *Reuben James* in the Atlantic.
l. Hitler seizes all of Czechoslovakia
m. Spanish civil war begins
n. Japan sends land forces into China
o. FDR and Churchill sign the Atlantic Charter

ANSWERS

II. True-False

1. True
2. True
3. False
4. False
5. False
6. True
7. False
8. True
9. True
10. True
11. False
12. False
13. True
14. True
15. False
16. False
17. True
18. True
19. True
20. False
21. False
22. False
23. True
24. False
25. True

III. Multiple Choice

1. b
2. a
3. d
4. c
5. a
6. b
7. d
8. c
9. c
10. b

IV. Fill-in

1. 29
2. 95%; no
3. munitions; Nye
4. third; scrap iron; oil
5. civil rights
6. lightning war
7. 3; 750,000
8. 43%; 80%
9. 35; rubber
10. 16%
11. $2; $15; $300
12. 8%
13. "Win-the-War"
14. 2,700
15. 1.1; 3.3
16. 96,000; 260
17. one
18. 6.9; 10.5
19. 50%
20. 290,000

VII. Chronology

a. 9
b. 6
c. 15
d. 3
e. 12
f. 8
g. 11
h. 1
i. 10
j. 2
k. 14
l. 7
m. 4
n. 5
o. 13

338

44

Fighting World War II
At the Pinnacle of Power
1942-1945

"the soft underbelly of Europe"

"Uncle Joe is killing more Germans and destroying more equipment than you and I put together."

"History never looks like history when you are living through it. It always looks confusing and messy, and it always feels uncomfortable."

John Gardner

I. Key Words

You should be able to define the following words and explain their historical significance in relation to the development of American history.

"Fortress Europe"
Pearl Harbor
D-Day
V-E Day and V-J Day
Admiral Yamamoto
General Douglas MacArthur
Bataan Peninsula
Corregidor Island
"I shall return."
Bataan Death March
Battle of the Coral Sea
Battle of Midway
aircraft carriers
issei, nissei, sansei
Earl Warren
Executive Order 9066
Korematsu v. the United States (1944)
"defeat Germany first" policy
second front
Sherman tank
General Erwin Rommel ("The Desert Fox")
Battle of Stalingrad

George Patton
Operation Overlord
General Dwight D. Eisenhower
Charles de Gaulle
Normandy
"Bloody Tarawa"
amphibious assault/amphibious warfare
V-2 rockets
Battle of the Bulge
unconditional surrender
Yalta conference
Chiang Kai-shek
Mao Zedong
Admiral Chester W. Nimitz
island-hopping strategy
incendiary bombing
Iwo Jima and Okinawa
Kamikaze tactics
Navajo "code talkers"
Manhattan Project
revisionist historians
J. Robert Oppenheimer
Harry S Truman
"Little Boy" and "Fat Man"
Hiroshima
Nagasaki

II. True-False

If the statement is false, change any words necessary to make it true.

1. Nazi Germany was defeated by Russian pluck, British technology, and American blood.

2. In contrast to the European war, the Pacific war was largely an American effort.

3. FDR ordered General Douglas MacArthur to stay in the Philippines with his soldiers and fight to the death, if necessary, to defend the islands.

4. After a quick strike at Pearl Harbor, Japanese policymakers hoped to negotiate a peace that would leave them in economic control of East Asia.

5. In the battle in the Coral Sea, American and Japanese warships pounded each other with heavy guns in the world's last close-range battleship duel.

6. The Japanese suffered a crucial defeat at Midway, losing aircraft carriers, airplanes (and experienced pilots) they could not replace.

7. If the Japanese had ever planned to invade California, it would most likely have been to attack William Randolph Hearst, the newspaper publisher who had been insulting them for 50 years.

8. Japan had to be defeated first, since Japan posed a greater threat to the American continent than Germany.

9. The Sherman tank, built in huge numbers during WWII, was easily the best tank in the war.

10. The military campaign in Italy, after the surrender of Italy, was relatively easy and ended in six months.

11. The "second front" that Stalin had demanded did not really come until Operation Overlord in June 1944, the largest amphibious invasion in world history.

12. Eisenhower had a dramatic military career and was a colorful, charismatic leader like Patton and MacArthur.

13. Eisenhower and his counterpart, British General Bernard Montgomery, agreed that the best way to defeat Germany was to concentrate all Allied forces into a single thrust into the heart of Germany—an "all-or-nothing" strategy.

14. American infantry divisions that fought their way from Normandy to Germany had at least a 100% replacement rate—combat replacements equaled the original number of troops assigned to the units.

15. The German V-2 rockets fired at London beginning in the summer of 1944 almost became the decisive weapon; they were the worst threat the Allies had to worry about for the rest of the war.

16. On April 30, 1945, Hitler was killed by a Russian mortar shell in his bunker in Berlin.

17. FDR, though in failing health at the Yalta conference, gave Stalin nothing that the Red Army had not already captured.

18. Douglas MacArthur was not particularly brave in battle, but he expected his soldiers to die without a whimper—and the casualties in his area of operations demonstrated that brutal fact.

19. As the war dragged on in the Pacific, Japanese soldiers became more willing to surrender.

20. The "island-hopping" strategy for the American advance in the Pacific gave the U.S. air bases from which to bomb the Japanese homeland.

21. U.S. submarines destroyed half of Japan's merchant ships within a few months.

22. Had the U.S. atomic bomb not ended the war, the U.S. planned to invade the Japanese homeland, beginning in November 1945.

23. The two atomic bombs ended WWII decisively and ahead of schedule.

24. Revisionist historians claim that the U.S. dropped the atomic bombs on Hiroshima and Nagasaki primarily to get revenge for the December 7th, 1941 attack on Pearl Harbor.

25. The casualty figures for the U.S. in WWII were the highest of any nation involved in the war on either side.

III. Multiple Choice

1. By early 1942, the Japanese had taken all but which of the following?

    a. Guam
    b. the Philippines
    c. Java
    d. Midway

2. The first battle that interrupted the steady drumbeat of Japanese victories in the Pacific was

    a. Wake Island
    b. Corregidor
    c. Singapore
    d. Coral Sea

3. In 1943, having cracked the Japanese naval code, Americans shot down the plane of

    a. Admiral Yamamoto
    b. General Tojo
    c. the most important Japanese spy
    d. General Harold, a Japanese double agent

4. People in the United States of Chinese and Korean descent in order to avoid physical attacks and to be identified as non-Japanese

    a. moved out of California
    b. wore Chinese clothing
    c. hired bodyguards of white background
    d. took to wearing identification buttons

5. The difference in the treatment of Japanese-Americans and the German-Americans was surprising since Germans practiced genocide, but Japan fought for

a. racial equality
b. the fulfillment of their nature
c. German purposes
d. economic domination of Asia

6. Stalin, because of Russia's horrendous casualties, demanded that the British and Americans

a. open a second front in Western Europe
b. send troops to Russia
c. negotiate an armistice
d. fight harder against the Germans

7. Prisoners of war (POWs) had greatly varying luck surviving their captivity. The least likely POW to return home from captivity was a

a. German captured by the Americans
b. American captured by the Germans
c. American captured by the Japanese
d. German captured by the Russians

8. FDR's Executive Order 9066

a. prohibited racial discrimination in war industries
b. prohibited racial segregation in the armed forces
c. established the Manhattan Project
d. defined coastal areas as forbidden to Japanese residence

9. The second front issue was finally resolved by

a. Operation Overlord
b. the invasion of North Africa
c. the invasion of Italy
d. American bombing of Germany from bases in England

10. The Normandy invasion (D-Day) was under the supreme command of

a. Bernard Montgomery
b. Winston Churchill
c. Dwight Eisenhower
d. George Patton

11. Had Japan not surrendered following the Nagasaki bomb, the anticipated next step in the war (November 1945) was to have been

a. the invasion of Okinawa
b. the assassination of the Japanese emperor
c. an amphibious assault on Japan itself
d. firebombing of civilian areas of Tokyo and other major Japanese cities

12. The consequence of the failure of the invasion of France was assumed to be

a. the loss of the war in Europe
b. failure to defeat Germany before the war in the Pacific would be over
c. Russian conquest of most of Western Europe
d. a minor setback in an otherwise successful military strategy

IV. Fill-in Questions

Fill in each blank in the following statements with the correct information.

1. The Soviet Union's war dead totaled _____ million during WWII.

2. MacArthur had _____ troops on the Bataan Peninsula and on Corregidor in December 1941.

3. Of 10,000 men who surrendered at Bataan, _____ died marching to prison camps and _____ men died in Japanese prison camps before the war was over.

4. About ____ percent of the Americans in Japanese POW camps died, compared to less than ____ percent for Americans in German camps.

5. The battle in Midway was more than a _____-for-_____ trade because the Japanese would have difficulty replacing their aircraft carrier losses.

6. Japan's offensive capacity was smashed just _____ months after Pearl Harbor.

7. About _____ Japanese (many of them American citizens) were forcibly removed from their homes and interned in "relocation camps" in _____ western states.

8. The internment policy cost Japanese-Americans their freedom for several years and about $_____ million in property. The government's policy was upheld in *Korematsu v. the United States* (1944) by a _____ to _____ Supreme Court decision.

9. In Hawaii about _____ of the population was of Japanese ancestry.

10. American and British bombers dropped _____ million tons of bombs on German cities.

11. Germany built _____ tanks during the war, but the U.S. built _____.

12. When the Battle of Stalingrad was over, Russians captured _____ of Hitler's best soldiers.

13. On D-Day, June 6th, 1944, _____ Allied soldiers came ashore at Normandy; by the end of June, there were _____ troops in France, and _____ vehicles.

14. The infantry divisions that fought from Normandy to Germany had a _____ percent replacement rate, and four divisions had a _____ percent replacement rate.

15. "Bloody Tarawa" was a stunning introduction to the fanaticism of its Japanese defenders. Of _____ Japanese on the atoll of Betio, only _____ surrendered.

16. V-2 rockets killed _____ people in London, and there was no defense against them.

17. MacArthur's troops made _____ amphibious landings, all of them successful.

18. After most of the remnants of the Japanese navy ceased to exist after the Battle of Leyte Gulf, the U.S. Navy had _____ ships.

19. *Kamikaze* suicide attacks at Okinawa sank _____ U.S. ships and damaged _____.

20. The military estimated that the invasion of Japan would cost _____ million casualties.

21. The Manhattan Project to build the American atomic bomb cost $_____ million.

22. The bomb dropped at Hiroshima killed _____ people in an instant and doomed another _____ to death from injury and radiation poisoning.

23. Over _____ million Americans were mobilized during the war.

24. The Second World War was the most expensive war the U.S. has ever fought, costing $_____ billion.

25. After the Nagasaki bomb was dropped, the U.S. had _____ more atomic bombs ready for use if the Japanese did not surrender.

V. Essay Questions

Write notes under each of the following questions that would help you answer similar essay questions on an exam.

1. Describe the beginning of the war in the Pacific. Was MacArthur's arrogance a necessary ingredient of successful leadership? Explain.

2. What was the significance of the battles of the Coral Sea and Midway? To what extent was this the "handwriting on the wall" for the Japanese, a strong indication that their war efforts would fail? Why?

3. Describe the treatment of Japanese-Americans early in WWII. Was this policy necessary?

4. What were the main characteristics of the North African campaign?

5. What were the main features of the Italian campaign? Could the African and Italian campaigns have been avoided and the Allies concentrated upon Germany itself? Why?

6. Describe D-Day, the invasion of Europe. Should the Allied forces have followed Montgomery's or Eisenhower's plan for the defeat of Germany? Explain.

7. Explain the Pacific strategy of the United States. Was it too costly? What other strategies could be been employed, given the geographic and military realities of the region?

8. Describe the making and use of the atomic bomb. What were the alternatives to using the bombs on two heavily populated cities? Why did Truman order the dropping of the Hiroshima and Nagasaki bombs? Summarize and evaluate the argument revisionist historians have made about Truman's decision.

9. What won the war for the Allies? Explain the particular strengths of each of the major participants in the war against Germany and Japan.

10. Discuss the role of technology in World War II. How broad a definition of "weapon" is appropriate?

ANSWERS

II. True-False

1. False
2. True
3. False
4. True
5. False
6. True
7. False
8. False
9. False
10. False
11. True
12. False
13. False
14. True
15. False
16. False
17. True
18. False
19. False
20. True
21. True
22. True
23. True
24. False
25. False

III. Multiple Choice

1. d
2. d
3. a
4. d
5. d
6. a
7. d
8. d
9. a
10. c
11. c
12. a

IV. Fill-in

1. 26
2. 20,000
3. 1,000; 5,000
4. 35%; 1%
5. one; four
6. seven
7. 110,000; seven
8. $350; six; three
9. one-third
10. 2.7
11. 8,000; 50,000
12. 250,000
13. 175,000; 450,000; 71,000
14. 100%; 200%
15. 5,000; 17
16. 8,000
17. 87
18. 4,000
19. 30; 300
20. 1
21. $2
22. 100,000; 100,000
23. 16
24. $560
25. no

45

Cold War
The U. S. in the Nuclear Age, 1946-1952

"containment"
"China Lobby"
"police action"
"Iron Curtain"

"History is baroque. It smiles at all attempts to force itself into theoretical patterns or logical grooves; it plays havoc with our generalizations, breaks all our rules."

Will Durant

I. Key Words

You should be able to define the following words and explain their historical significance in relation to the development of American history.

Hiroshima and Nagasaki
legacies of WWII
genocide
Dachau, Belsen, Auschwitz, and Buchenwald
Cold War
Bolsheviks of 1917
GI Bill of Rights
Katyn massacre
Polish question
Winston Churchill
"Iron Curtain" speech, 1946
52-20 Club
George F. Kennan ("Mister X")
Containment policy
Truman Doctrine
George C. Marshall
Marshall Plan
United Nations
Berlin blockade and airlift, 1948
North Atlantic Treaty Organization (NATO, 1949)

Warsaw Pact
Taft-Hartley Act of 1947
Wagner Act of 1935
Eightieth Congress
Truman's "Fair Deal"
"Jim Crow" laws
Henry A. Wallace
Strom Thurmond
"Dixiecrats"
Thomas E. Dewey
"Give 'em hell, Harry!"
Chiang Kai-shek
Mao Tse-tung
Joseph "Vinegar Joe" Stilwell
China Lobby
"unleashing" Chiang Kai-shek
Dean Acheson
Republic of Korea
UN "police action" in Korea
Inchon invasion
ROKs
Douglas MacArthur
Panmunjom
"twenty years of treason"
loyalty oaths and security risks
"red baiting"
Alger Hiss
Whittaker Chambers
Richard Nixon
Joseph McCarthy
McCarthyism
McCarran Internal Security Act
Dennis et al. v. United States (1951)
Dwight D. Eisenhower
Adlai Stevenson

II. True-False

If the statement is false, change any words necessary to make it true.

1. The second legacy of the war was the discovery that reports of genocide in German Europe had not been exaggerated.

2. The only two genuine victors of WWII were the Americans and their British allies.

3. The origins of the Cold War lay in the nature of Communist ideology—dating back to 1917—which was fundamentally incompatible with the American commitment to democratic government and individual liberties.

4. U.S. recognition of the Soviet Union in 1933 was prompted by practical thinking, including the hope that American exports might increase, rather than by any liking for communism.

5. Like FDR, Truman liked Joseph Stalin personally and thought he could cooperate with him in the postwar world.

6. More pessimistic than Truman, George Kennan, a State Department expert on the Soviet Union, said the only way to deal with what he called the "Russkies" was to make war on them before they could recover from WWII or build their own atomic weapons.

7. The most serious challenge to the containment policy in Europe was the 1948 blockade of Berlin, caused by France's refusal to agree to a rearmed West Germany.

8. "Had Enough?" was President Truman's campaign slogan in 1948, directed at the Republicans who controlled both houses of Congress.

9. The Taft-Hartley Labor-Management Relations Act of 1947 reversed the New Deal's support of organized labor and emphasized the right of employees not to join a union.

10. Most political experts thought Truman would win in 1948.

11. The Soviet expansionism that was responsible in part for the Cold War in Europe did not lie at the bottom of Communist successes in China.

12. Before the Chinese intervened in the Korean War, United Nations forces had occupied nearly all of North Korea (after a disastrous start of the war.)

13. The Chinese in the Korean War protected their borders and the Americans had ensured the independence of the Republic of Korea.

14. When MacArthur returned after his dismissal, he established residence in New York and issued political proclamations.

15. The chief beneficiaries of the "twenty years of treason" scare were Joseph McCarthy and Richard Nixon.

16. Joseph McCarthy claimed he had a list of 205 Communists who were working in the State Department, and two days later claimed the list had 57 names on it, but when he finally produced the list, there were actually over 500 names.

17. McCarthy's downfall came in 1954 when he accused the U.S. army of being infiltrated by Communists.

18. Dwight Eisenhower was a lifelong Republican politician, and so was the ideal choice to head that party's presidential ticket in 1952.

19. Adlai Stevenson, Eisenhower's opponent in 1952, had been Truman's vice president, and was tainted by allegations of corruption and inefficiency in the Truman administration.

20. The Chinese agreed to end the Korean War in 1953 after Eisenhower ordered one small atomic bomb to be used on the Chinese troops in Korea.

III. Multiple Choice

1. Polish hatred for the Russians was given new life in 1943 when the Germans released evidence that the Red Army had secretly massacred five thousand captured

    a. Jews
    b. German civilians
    c. Polish officers
    d. Catholic priests

2. The principle of supporting anti-Communist governments with military aid came to be known as

    a. the Truman Doctrine
    b. the United Front
    c. the Truman Campaign
    d. the Cold War

3. By late 1947, Stalin's troops were in control of Eastern Europe including the nation with a strong democratic tradition

    a. Poland
    b. Germany
    c. Czechoslovakia
    d. Ukraine

4. The Soviets responded to the establishment of NATO by

    a. blockading Berlin
    b. invading Czechoslovakia
    c. withdrawing from Germany
    d. organizing the Warsaw Pact

5. Since enemies knocked his homey and common appearance, Truman decided to

a. seek help from image-makers
b. become the common man
c. read and attend cultural events
d. make few public appearances

6. What did Truman ban in the armed forces, in the civil service, and in companies that did business with the federal government?

a. firing for political reasons
b. elaborate regulations and tests
c. expenditure of unappropriated funds
d. racial discrimination

7. Henry A. Wallace claimed to be the true heir of the New Deal and insisted that the United States

a. continue friendship with the Soviet Union
b. occupy Western Europe
c. form aid centers for Africa and Asia
d. push the Soviet Union back to its borders

8. "Mr. X" was the (temporary) pen name of

a. "The Man Nobody Knows"
b. George C. Marshall
c. Winston Churchill
d. George Kennan

9. The outcome of the Berlin crisis of 1948 was

a. division of the city into East Berlin and West Berlin
b. the first failure of the containment policy
c. the Berlin Airlift
d. all of these

10. Which of these 1948 candidates did not come from the Democratic Party?

a. Thomas E. Dewey
b. Strom Thurmond
c. Henry A. Wallace
d. Harry S Truman

IV. Fill-in Questions

Fill in each blank in the following statements with the correct information.

1. The Nazis had systematically exterminated _____ million Jews and probably _____ million others in camps specifically designed for killing.

2. Of _____ million men and women eligible to attend college free under the GI Bill, _____ million actually did.

3. Members of the 52-20 Club of 1945 and 1946 were unemployed, demobilized soldiers and sailors who were allowed $_____ a week for _____ weeks. .

4. According to Winston Churchill in a famous 1946 speech, an "_____" had descended across Europe.

5. Truman asked Congress to appropriate $_____ million in military assistance to the pro-Western governments of Greece and Turkey.

6. The U.S. gave Marshall Plan assistance to _____ nations; Churchill called the Marshall Plan "the most _____ act in history."

7. During the Berlin Airlift of 1948, there were more than _____ flights carrying _____ million tons of good into Berlin.

8. In April 1949, the United States signed a treaty with Canada and _____ European nations establishing NATO.

9. Truman vetoed over _____ anti-New Deal bills passed by Congress.

10. Truman won the 1948 election with a _____ to _____ electoral vote margin, despite having _____ opponents who had bolted from the Democratic party to run against him.

11. The division of Korea was along the _____ parallel of latitude.

12. After the invasion of North Korea at Inchon, American forces cut off and captured _____ North Korean troops, and took back all of South Korea in just _____ weeks, but then _____ sent _____ troops into the war, pushing the U.S. back.

13. Defense expenditures soared from _____ billion in 1950 to $_____ billion in 1952.

14. The Korean War killed nearly _____ Americans.

15. Joseph McCarthy's investigations eventually found _____ Communists in the federal government. He was censured by the U.S. Senate by a vote of _____ to _____, becoming only the _____ senator to be thus disciplined.

16. In 1952 Eisenhower won _____ percent of the popular vote and _____ electoral votes to Stevenson's ____.

V. Essay Questions

Write notes under each of the following questions that would help you answer similar essay questions on an exam.

1. What were the three legacies of the Cold War? Which was the most important? Why? Were these legacies more ominous than those of World War I? Explain.

2. How much cooperation was there between the Soviet Union and the United States during WWII? What histories in each country would tend to limit cooperation other than as a wartime necessity? Should the start (or resumption) of the Cold War have been a surprise, once the threats of Germany and Japan were removed?

3. Explain the roots and early stages of Soviet-American animosity. To what extent were the antagonisms a lack of understanding and communication rather than a real threat?

4. What was the "Iron Curtain"?

5. Describe the containment policy. On what assumptions did it rest, and how well did it work? Was Kennan's view of Soviet behavior valid?

6. What were the similarities and the difference between the Truman Doctrine and the Marshall Plan? Could these programs work together, or were they mutually exclusive?

7. Compare the Marshall Plan for Europe with the victors' attitude and behavior after World War I. Is this an example of policymakers learning from history? Why or why not?

8. Describe Truman's domestic political policy. What was the Fair Deal?

9. Was Truman looking for votes in his civil rights policy or was he risking votes by his support of blacks? Explain.

10. Describe the election of 1948. How can you explain the Truman victory? Would scientific polling techniques of today have overcome the expectation that Dewey would win the election?

11. Explain the choices in the United States' China policy after the Second World War. Considering what has happened since that time, would we have been better off to become friends with Mao back in the 1940s? Why? Is an organization like the "China Lobby" dangerous? Explain.

12. What are the important events and decisions in the Korean War? Could the war have been prevented? Explain.

13. Why did Truman fire Douglas MacArthur? Describe the background, the immediate situation that convinced Truman to dismiss him, and the eventual result.

14. Describe in detail the years of charges of treason and subversion within the United States. Is McCarthyism un-American? Why or why not? Was the era of McCarthy an unusual period in our history or one likely to occur again and again? Explain.

15. What were the essential features of the 1952 election? Was Eisenhower a good choice for president?

ANSWERS

II. True-False

1. True
2. False
3. True
4. True
5. False
6. False
7. False
8. False
9. True
10. False
11. True
12. True
13. True
14. True
15. True
16. False
17. True
18. False
19. False
20. False

III. Multiple Choice

1. c
2. a
3. c
4. d
5. b
6. d
7. a
8. d
9. c
10. a

IV. Fill-in

1. 6; 1
2. 14; 2.2
3. $20; 52
4. "Iron Curtain"
5. $400
6. 16; "unsordid"
7. 250,000; 2
8. nine
9. 80
10. 303; 189; two
11. 38th
12. 100,000; two; China; 200,000
13. $40; $71
14. 37,000
15. no (0); 72; 22; third
16. 55%; 442; 89

46

Eisenhower Country
American Life in the 1950s

"Enjoy yourself, it's later than you think."

"one-eyed monster"

"Keep up with the Joneses"

"He is the happiest of whom the world says least, good or bad."

Thomas Jefferson

I.   Key Words

You should be able to define the following words and explain their historical significance in relation to the development of American history.

Dwight D. Eisenhower
Sherman Adams
Jonas Salk
Davy Crockett, "hula hoops," Barbie dolls (and other toy fads)
television ("boob-tube")
Ronald Reagan
Disneyland
suburbia
Levittown
William Levitt
conformism
the automobile economy
Interstate Highway Act of 1956
the baby boom
democratization of fashion
Christian Dior
rock 'n' roll
Elvis Presley
changing roles for women
Alfred Kinsey
Betty Friedan and *The Feminine Mystique*
The Organization Man
beatniks
NAACP

Plessy v. Ferguson
Thurgood Marshall
Brown v. Board of Education of Topeka
Orval Faubus
Earl Warren
Martin Luther King, Jr.
Rosa Parks
Southern Christian Leadership Conference (SCLC)
Student Nonviolent Coordinating Committee (SNCC)
"freedom riders"

II. True-False

If the statement is false, change any words necessary to make it true.

1. The voters of 1952 wanted a change of pace, but no upheaval; they wanted new faces in government, but did not want to repeal the New Deal.

2. Eisenhower disliked reading more than a page on any subject, a "brief," such as he had dealt with in the army.

3. The majority of Americans did not object to a president who enjoyed himself.

4. In the 1950s, there had been a remarkable shift in the distribution of wealth.

5. America in the 1950s was vastly richer as a result of the extraordinary economic growth of the Second World War decade.

6. Still remembering the Great Depression and the hardships of World War II, the 1950s generation tended to "save for a rainy day," and had to be persuaded to buy most consumer goods.

7. More Americans knew the name of the French clothing designer Christian Dior than could name the plumber in Eisenhower's cabinet.

8. By 1970, more American households were equipped with a television set than had refrigerators, bathtubs, or indoor toilets.

9. The "one-eyed monster" drastically changed the reading habits of older Americans.

10. The cultural tone of the 1950s was set by suburbanites—residents of the new middle-class automobile suburbs built after the war.

11. There was a racial component—"white flight"—to the shift from city to suburbs, a postwar response to the influx of southern blacks to northern cities.

12. Every house in Levittown was exactly like all the others the Levitts made; like Henry Ford's Model T, there was only one design, and all houses were even painted the same color.

13. By 1960, as many Americans lived in suburbs as in large cities.

14. Suburbanites, having mostly come from the cities where the Democratic party was dominant, remained true to the Democratic party.

15. The yard and house were the most important means by which people displayed their economic and social status in the 1950s.

16. Rock-'n'-roll music was based on the rhythms of black music.

17. "Rosie the Riveter" erased forever the line between what men did and what women did; "Rosie" was the first symbol of feminism, since women war workers, once employed outside the home, almost always stayed on in the workforce after the war was over.

18. Beatniks rebelled against what they considered to be the intellectually and socially stultifying aspects of 1950s America.

19. The beatniks introduced marijuana to white America.

20. Lynching, once a weekly occurrence in the South and only rarely punished, almost disappeared in the 1950s.

21. The Supreme Court declared in *Brown v. Board of Education* that racially separate public facilities were constitutional as long as they were equal in quality.

22. President Eisenhower privately blamed the racial disturbances in Little Rock, Arkansas, in 1957 on Earl Warren, whose Supreme Court had ruled against school segregation in *Brown v. Board of Education.*

23. After his home was bombed, Martin Luther King, Jr., renounced his original policy of nonviolence and called for southern blacks to adopt "an eye for an eye" as the strategy for forcing racial change on America.

24. African Americans had to wait until the 1960s to see any progress in race relations.

25. Children born in the 1940s and 1950s were the first generation of Americans to grow up with television.

III. Multiple Choice

1. Eisenhower's style was calculated to

   a. deaden
   b. soothe
   c. disrupt
   d. put fear in opponents

2. To some extent, the numerous manias of the 1950s were instigated and promoted by the

   a. advertising industry
   b. lack of serious problems
   c. worldwide prosperity
   d. search for novelty

3. The home television receiver became one of the greatest forces for

   a. good
   b. national unity
   c. education
   d. conformism

4. The television show, "Death Valley Days," revived the career of

   a. John Wayne
   b. Elizabeth Taylor
   c. Ronald Reagan
   d. Matt Dillon

5. Because networks preferred announcers who spoke "standard American English"

   a. talent searches were nationwide
   b. regional variations in speech declined
   c. southern stations refused to join networks
   d. emphasis was put on accent over ability

6. The supermarkets encouraged weekly rather than daily shopping thus eliminating

   a. waste
   b. need for cars
   c. additional occasions for social life
   d. small groceries

7. Since everyone was a stranger in the new suburban towns, the efficient means by which to introduce people to one another was the

a. cocktail party
b. Little League game
c. coffee sessions
d. recreation night

8. Mattel became the nation's 4th largest producer of clothing because of the popularity of

a. "Davy Crockett" outfits
b. "Barbie" dolls
c. "poodle" skirts
d. the "Beatnik look"

9. The 1950s suburbs could not have developed without

a. William Levitt
b. shopping malls
c. the automobile
d. advertising

10. Until driven off the air by the whiff of scandal, one of the most popular forms of 1950s television entertainment was

a. soap operas
b. "shoot-'em-up" westerns
c. variety shows
d. quiz shows

IV. Fill-in Questions

Fill in each blank in the following statements with the correct information.

1. "_____ millionaires and a plumber," a Democrat sniffed about Eisenhower's cabinet.

2. The wealthiest _____ percent of the population enjoyed more than _____ percent of the national income.

3. In 1940, discretionary income—money left over after rent, food, and other necessities are paid for—was $_____ billion; in 1950, discretionary income was $_____ billion.

4. By 1965, one-fourth of the U.S. population (statistically) had gone to _____.

5. In less than a year, Americans spent more than $_____ million in memory of Davy Crockett.

6. Almost immediately, _____ million "hula hoops" were sold for $1.98 each.

7. Because of the popularity of the "Barbie" doll, the nation's fourth largest manufacturer of "women's clothing was actually a _____ company, Mattel.

8. One of the short-lived fads of the 1950s was the addition of "green stuff," or _____ to about 90 products. Before the fad ended, Americans had spent $_____ million on the products.

9. In 1946, there were only _____ privately owned television receivers in the United States. By 1950, almost _____ million sets had been sold, one for every _____ people in the country.

10. One _____ of prime time television viewing hours were filled by Wild West dramas.

11. The networks tried out _____ dramas set in the Wild West. "Gunsmoke" ran through _____ half-hour episodes seen (at least one program) by _____ percent of the world's population.

12. Purchase of books increased by _____ percent from 1940s to the 1950s.

13. There were _____ million housing starts in 1946 and _____ million in 1950, the vast majority in the suburbs.

14. The population of the new suburban communities was _____ percent white, young married couples with infant children.

15. One suburban family in _____ owned two automobiles. From zero sales of automobiles during the war, sales rose to _____ million in 1950. By 1960, car ownership was almost _____ million.

16. Short-term debt—money borrowed to buy consumer goods—increased from $_____ billion in 1946 to $_____ billion in 1970.

17. In 1945 there were _____ automobile-oriented shopping centers in the United States, but by 1960 there were almost _____.

18. The government spent $____ billion a year (and later $____ billion a year) to construct _____ miles of new cross-country interstate highways.

19. ____ million babies were born in 1946, compared to about _____ million a year in the 1930s. The "baby boom" continued to increase until _____, when _____ million were born.

20. Middle-class teenagers had $_____ billion of their own to spend each year in the 1950s.

21. In 1953, only _____ states explicitly prohibited racial segregation.

V. Essay Questions

Write notes under each of the following questions that would help you answer similar essay questions on an exam.

1. Describe Ike's style as president. Was Eisenhower the kind of president the founding fathers envisioned? Explain.

2. What were the signs of enjoyment and fun in the 1950s? Would you consider this period a decline in American society or one of fulfillment? Why?

3. In what ways did television affect American life in the 1950s? Does TV still have the same influences? Explain. Generally, were the results of the introduction of television on a massive scale harmful, beneficial, or neutral in its impact on American life? Explain.

4. Describe suburbia. What was the social impact of the emergence of suburbs? Overall, was this change beneficial or harmful? Explain.

5. What were the features of the automobile economy? Would a modern, efficient public transportation system have been better than the explosion of automobiles? Why or why not?

6. What social developments regarding population and women occurred in the 1950s? Was this a period of liberation for women? Explain.

7. Explain the viewpoints of the dissenters to the suburban, middle-class conformist style of life.

8. Describe the early black rights movement. What was Eisenhower's position on *Brown v. Board of Education*? Was Eisenhower being a good president by enforcing a decision with which he did not agree? Explain.

9. Explain the views of Martin Luther King, Jr., on nonviolent civil disobedience. Was this strategy usually effective? Explain.

10. Describe the fashions of the fifties. Should a history textbook include discussion of fashions? Why or why not?

ANSWERS

II. True-False

1. True
2. True
3. True
4. False
5. True
6. False
7. True
8. True
9. False
10. True
11. True
12. False
13. True
14. False
15. False
16. True
17. False
18. True
19. True
20. True
21. False
22. True
23. False
24. False
25. True

IV. Fill-in

1. Eight
2. 20; 44
3. $40; $100
4. Disneyland
5. $100
6. 30
7. toy
8. chlorophyll; $135
9. 8,000; 4; 32
10. third
11. 40; 635; 25%
12. 53%
13. 1; 2
14. 95%
15. five; 6.7; 62
16. $8; $127
17. 8; 4,000
18. 1; 2.9; 41,000
19. 3.4; 2.5; 1961; 4.2
20. $10
21. 15

III. Multiple Choice

1. b
2. a
3. d
4. c
5. b
6. c
7. a
8. b
9. c
10. d

47

Ike and Camelot
Policies Under Eisenhower and Kennedy
1953-1963

"The torch has been passed to a new generation of Americans."

"Ask not what your country can do for you; ask what you can do for your country."

John F. Kennedy

"Some are so very studious of learning what was done by the ancients that they know not how to live with the moderns."

William Penn

I. Key Words

You should be able to define the following words and explain their historical significance in relation to the development of American history.

Jonas Salk
Soil Bank Act of 1956
Tennessee Valley Authority
"creeping socialism"
"military-industrial complex"
"dynamic conservatism"
Cold War
"massive retaliation"
"more bang for a buck"
fallout shelters
"military-industrial complex"
peaceful coexistence
Nikita Khrushchev
John Foster Dulles
Third World
Allen Dulles
Central Intelligence Agency
Dulles's "us and them" view of foreign policy
Central Intelligence Agency (CIA)

Geneva Accords
Vietnam
anticolonialism
"brinkmanship"
Hungarian revolt (1956)
Suez Canal crisis
U-2 crisis
Francis Gary Powers
John F. Kennedy
22nd Amendment
Richard Nixon
Lyndon Johnson
"Camelot"
the New Frontier
Peace Corps
Congress of Racial Equality (CORE)
"freedom riders"
Medgar Evers
Robert F. Kennedy
1963 March on Washington
Martin Luther King, Jr.
"flexible response" policy
Green Berets
Bay of Pigs invasion
Berlin Wall
1962 Cuban missile crisis
nuclear test ban treaty
Lee Harvey Oswald
John Birch Society
Warren Commission

II.   True-False

If the statement is false, change any words necessary to make it true.

1. Since 1963, Americans have had more confidence in themselves and in the people who run the country than before 1963.

2. President Eisenhower was troubled by the expansion of the federal government during the New Deal and WWII, and believed that businessmen in the private sector were better qualified to manage the economy than Washington's bureaucrats were.

3. Despite occasional evidence of a pragmatic attitude, Eisenhower at heart was a conservative ideologue and a lifelong right-wing conservative.

4. When the Salk polio vaccine was perfected, the Secretary of Health, Education, and Welfare warned that even if the program would wipe out disease, for the government to sponsor it would be socialistic.

5. Eisenhower called the Tennessee Valley Authority "creeping socialism" and ordered that it be sold off to private investors.

6. Every president between Truman and Clinton had to shape their foreign policies around the fact of U.S.-Soviet confrontation.

7. NATO's conventional forces easily outnumbered those of the Warsaw Pact, its Soviet-sponsored opposing alliance.

8. As president, Eisenhower, old army man that he was, saw to it that the Army's budget was higher than that of the Navy or Air Force.

9. The U.S. was involved in no significant military action during Eisenhower's eight years in office.

10. The term "Third World" was 1950s diplomatic shorthand for those nations allied with the United States, but not sharing an American standard of living.

11. John Foster Dulles served in the Eisenhower administration both as secretary of state and director of the CIA.

12. The U.S. did not intervene in the Hungarian crisis, even though American propaganda broadcasts to Eastern Europe had broadly implied that the U.S. would help nations rebel against the Soviets.

13. The U-2 incident of 1960, in which an American plane was shot down over Russia, would have been much more serious if the pilot had lived to confess that he was on a spying mission, not a weather flight.

14. The "missile gap" was the discovery that the Soviets had bigger, better, and many more rockets than the U.S. possessed.

15. John F. Kennedy was not only younger than most presidents had been at the time of his taking office, but he was much healthier than nearly all others.

16. Kennedy's personal popularity and his impressive performance in the four presidential debates (as well as Nixon's unpopularity) made JFK's landslide victory in 1960 a foregone conclusion.

17. "Vigor" was a favorite Kennedy word.

18. Kennedy knew the U.S. was behind the Soviets in the space race (the first earth-orbiting unmanned satellite was put in space by the Russians in 1957), but he meant to put an American on the moon within ten years.

19. Even after the 1963 March on Washington, Kennedy refused to enforce existing civil rights laws or support proposals for new legislation, since he did not want to alienate southern segregationists in his own party.

20. Kennedy believed that the Cuban missile crisis was the turning point in his presidency.

III. Multiple Choice

1. Both Eisenhower and Kennedy enjoyed something that none of their successors did. This was

a. war in Asia
b. a balanced budget
c. a consensus, the belief that all is well
d. the expansion of the United States

2. Eisenhower publicly denounced the Tennessee Valley Authority as

a. communist
b. creeping socialism
c. a devilish plot
d. the work of "un-American radicals"

3. As agricultural production outstripped demand,

a. farm subsidies were increased
b. farm subsidies decreased slightly
c. farm subsidies were decreased significantly, to force extra farmers off the land
d. the Eisenhower administration adopted a "sink-or-swim" attitude toward farmers, removing all subsidies and essentially putting the Department of Agriculture as well as many farmers out of business.

4. Because the two powers were nuclear superpowers, the Cold War contest could not be resolved by the timeless test of

a. negotiation
b. power politics
c. alliances
d. decisive war

5. In Kennedy's policy of flexible response, the United States would

a. blow up Moscow
b. respond according to the seriousness of the crisis
c. ignore the USSR
d. use flexible weapons

6. In 1954 the CIA took the lead in overthrowing a democratically chosen prime minister in Guatemala because he

a. burned the American flag
b. believed in a socialist economic system
c. expropriated American-owned banana plantations
d. insulted Dulles at an airport meeting

7. Eisenhower assumed that the U-2 pilot was dead because

a. the pilot was supposed to commit suicide if shot down
b. no one could survive in the air at that height
c. the plane would explode completely if it were hit
d. Khrushchev would show the pilot at once if he were still alive

8. Which of these countries was considered part of the Third World in the 1950s?

a. India
b. China
c. United Kingdom
d. Soviet Union

9. The U-2 was

a. a long-range weather-monitoring airplane
b. a top-secret high-altitude spy plane
c. the first earth-orbiting satellite
d. an atomic-powered American bomber

10. "Tricky Dicky" was a nickname for

a. Richard E. Daley, mayor of Chicago
b. Richard Hollingshead, inventor of the drive-in movie
c. Richard Nixon, 1960 presidential candidate
d. none of these

IV. Fill-in Questions

Fill in each blank in the following statements with the correct information.

1. By 1966 $_____ of every $_____ that farmers and agricultural corporations pocketed at harvest time came from the federal government for crops that were never planted.

2. In 1957 and 1958, a recession threw _____ percent of the work force out of jobs, so Ike launched several large public-works projects.

3. Over ____ million names were added to the lists of people who received Social Security during Eisenhower's presidency.

4. A professional built fallout shelter cost $_____ in the 1950s.

5. As late as 1940, there were still _____ acres of farmland within the city limits of Philadelphia.

6. A ranch house in Levittown could be bought for as little as $_____.

7. In 1940 there were only _____ supermarkets in the U.S., one for every _____ people; by 1960, there were _____, one for every _____ people.

8. Between 1945 and 1950, _____ drive-in movie theaters were built.

9. John Foster Dulles flew _____ miles on the job as secretary of state.

10. As a slap at Franklin Roosevelt, Republicans pushed through the _____ Amendment to limit presidents to two terms.

11. Kennedy won the 1960 election by _____ votes out of almost _____ million cast.

12. Kennedy's space program was going to put a man on the _____ by _____.

13. According to Kennedy, Washington, D.C., was "a city of southern _____ and northern _____."

14. Kennedy sent _____ marshals and _____ soldiers, at a cost of $_____ million, to ensure that one black man, James Meredith, could attend the University of Mississippi.

15. James Baldwin said, regarding racial prejudice, that it was a shock at the age of five or six to find out that in a world of Gary Coopers you are the _____.

16. In August 1963, Martin Luther King, Jr., led _____ supporters to the Lincoln Memorial in Washington where he delivered his "I Have a _____" speech.

17. The CIA had _____ agents around the world.

18. The Soviet Union had _____ intercontinental missiles in Cuba and _____ on the way there in 1962. There were also _____ Russian troops in Cuba.

19. After the Cuban missile crisis, the Soviet Union joined the U.S. and United Kingdom in signing a treaty that banned _____ in the atmosphere.

20. Texas was home to several paranoiac right-wing political organizations, including the _____ Society, which called Eisenhower a "conscious agent" of international Communism.

V. Essay Questions

Write notes under each of the following questions that would help you answer similar essay questions on an exam.

1. Explain the actual views of Eisenhower and then his process of compromise with reality. Is this a common experience of a president—principles and attitudes that eventually have to be compromised when decisions related to reality must be made? Should that procedure take place? Why?

2. Describe Eisenhower's foreign policy plans. What was wrong with the policy of "massive retaliation"?

3. What were the weaknesses of John Foster Dulles as Secretary of State? How might future international problems have been avoided if Eisenhower had appointed a more reasonable and practical Secretary of State? Be specific. Was a golden opportunity for a friendlier relationship with the USSR lost in the 1950s? Explain.

4. Explain how the United States "picked the wrong friends" in this period. Is this still a problem of American foreign policy? Explain with appropriate examples.

5. Describe the U-2 incident. Would it have been better for Eisenhower to deny knowledge of the spy plane? Why or why not?

6. What were the issues and the new factors to appear in the 1960 election? Why was Kennedy able to win? How important were the presidential debates in the outcome of the election?

7. In what ways was Kennedy a great president? In what ways might he be considered a failure?

8. Explain the various views of the assassination of Kennedy.

9. Was Kennedy's foreign policy a success? Consider "flexible response," the Bay of Pigs invasion, and the Cuban missile crisis.

10. Describe and evaluate Kennedy's civil rights record. Were John Kennedy and his brother Robert, the Attorney General, civil rights leaders, or were they forced by circumstances to respond to challenges in the South?

ANSWERS

II. True-False

1. False
2. True
3. False
4. True
5. False
6. True
7. False
8. False
9. True
10. False
11. False
12. True
13. False
14. False
15. False
16. False
17. True
18. True
19. False
20. True

III. Multiple Choice

1. c
2. b
3. a
4. d
5. b
6. c
7. a
8. a
9. b
10. c

IV. Fill-in

1. 1; 6
2. 7%
3. 10
4. $3,000
5. 10,000
6. $9,900
7. 6,000; 22,000; 33,000; 5,400
8. 5,000
9. 500,000
10. 22nd
11. 118,574; 70
12. moon; 1970
13. efficiency; charm
14. 400; 300; $4
15. Indian
16. 200,000; Dream
17. 15,000
18. 20; 20; 40,000
19. nuclear testing
20. John Birch

48

Johnson's Great Society Reform and Conflict 1961-1968

"True, there is government harassment, but there still is that relative freedom to fight. I can attack my government, try to change it. That's more than I can do in Moscow, Peking, or Havana."

Saul Alinsky

"To be ignorant of what happened before you were born is to be ever a child. For what is man's lifetime unless the memory of past events is woven with those of earlier times."

Cicero

I. Key Words

You should be able to define the following words and explain their historical significance in relation to the development of American history.

Lyndon Baines Johnson (LBJ)
Sam Rayburn
the "Johnson treatment"
the Great Society
Civil Rights Act of 1964
Jim Crow laws
Student Nonviolent Coordinating Committee (SNCC, or "Snick")
Freedom Summer
Mississippi Freedom Democratic Party
Fannie Lou Hamer
Hubert Humphrey
Barry Goldwater
Voting Rights Act of 1965
War on Poverty
Office of Economic Opportunity (OEO)
Job Corps
Volunteers in Service to America (VISTA)
Indochina (Vietnam, Laos, and Cambodia)
Ho Chi Minh
Viet Minh

Dien Bien Phu
Geneva Accords of 1954
China Lobby
Ngo Dinh Diem
National Liberation Front (NLF)
Vietcong
Army of the Republic of Vietnam (ARVN)
Green Berets
"domino theory"
Gulf of Tonkin Resolution
defoliation
General William Westmoreland
Tet Offensive
hawks and doves
My Lai massacre
"black power"
Malcolm Little (Malcolm X)
Nation of Islam
Stokely Carmichael
SNCC
Black Panthers
Students for a Democratic Society (SDS)
Port Huron Statement
the "New Left"
Berkeley Free Speech Movement
"counterculture"
Eugene McCarthy
Robert F. Kennedy
George Wallace
"white backlash" vote
Kevin Phillips

II.　True-False

If the statement is false, change any words necessary to make it true.

1. Lyndon Johnson liked his initials so much that he named his two daughters and renamed his wife so their initials would also be LBJ.

2. LBJ grew up near the University of Texas and attended it after attending high school in a rural town.

3. Johnson's election to the Senate in 1948 was by such a large majority that he picked up the nickname "Landslide Lyndon."

4. The "Johnson treatment" was a combination of syrupy Texas charm, legislative favors, and, when necessary, blackmail.

5. Johnson's first presidential act was a tax cut.

6. Johnson was a nominal supporter of segregation as late as 1960.

7. Rural and provincial, many southern blacks were suspicious of outsiders during the 1964 "Freedom Summer."

8. Mississippi's white delegation to the 1964 Democratic convention walked out when the party allowed some representation to the Mississippi Freedom Democratic party.

9. A Democratic television spot aimed at Goldwater depicted a little girl playing in a field of wild flowers and dissolved into a film of a nuclear blast.

10. Barry Goldwater was personally temperate, but he allied himself with right-wing extremists in 1964, including the John Birch Society, which believed that Communists were in charge of the federal and state governments.

11. The Voting Rights Act of 1965 put the states' power of enforcement behind the right of blacks to vote.

12. George Wallace, who as a 1960s governor of Alabama had promised "segregation forever," asked for and received black votes in 1982.

13. Johnson disliked Roosevelt and the New Deal, but he began programs to help the poor for political purposes.

14. The corruption, waste, inefficiency and high cost of Johnson's Great Society programs destroyed his administration.

15. Ho Chi Minh proclaimed Vietnam's independence in 1945, using words from the American Declaration of Independence.

16. Though Vietnam would become the most unpopular war in modern memory, only two senators voted in 1964 against allowing Johnson to "take all necessary measures" to protect American interests in Vietnam.

17. The Tet Offensive was both a political and a military victory for the Vietcong and North Vietnamese.

18. At My Lai in March 1968, American troops killed 347 unarmed men, women, and children.

19. "Black power" was never clearly defined, but for most African Americans, it meant demanding a part of the United States to be set aside for blacks to form a separate nation.

20. Malcolm X was gunned down by Black Muslim assassins in 1965.

21. The various communes founded by "flower children" in the 1960s proved to be the longest-lasting legacy of the counterculture.

22. LBJ wanted to run again in 1968, but he faced a rebellion within his Democratic party, and he was denied the nomination in a heated convention.

23. George Wallace gained support in the North as well as among white southerners, and was the chief threat to a Nixon victory in 1968.

24. As expected, Wallace's third party forced the 1968 election into the House of Representatives when the Electoral College could not decide on the winner.

25. Kevin Phillips predicted—correctly—that the Republican party would be the dominant party at the end of the 20th century.

III. Multiple Choice

1. Johnson was good at being a master assembler of

   a. Democratic patronage
   b. Southern votes for the president
   c. farm and worker support
   d. Senate majorities

2. The most stubborn of the segregated states was

   a. Georgia
   b. Mississippi
   c. Alabama
   d. Texas

3. Goldwater seemed to say that the Cold War with the Soviet Union was a matter of

   a. which country was "tougher"
   b. military determination
   c. talking the other side out of its positions
   d. ignoring the other side

4. During the 1970s, Atlanta, New Orleans, Newark, Gary, and Detroit all

   a. went deeply into debt
   b. acquired professional sports teams
   c. elected black mayors
   d. opened black industries to compete with white

5. Students during the 1960s did not

a. demonstrate against capital punishment
b. support the House of Un-American Activities Committee
c. work in the civil-rights movement
d. oppose violations of civil liberties

6. By 1968 the daily cost of the war in Vietnam had risen to

a. $70 million
b. $25 billion
c. $700 thousand
d. $70 thousand

7. While the majority of blacks supported the Great Society, many young militants attacked the president's integrationist policies in the name of

a. God
b. the black-power movement
c. the black gospel
d. the expense and thus increased taxes

8. Kevin Phillips predicted in 1968 that which political party would become dominant by the end of the century?

a. Democrats
b. Republicans
c. Independents
d. Black Nationalists

9. The most effective 1964 televised political ad implied that the Republican presidential candidate was

a. a racist
b. too old
c. a "flower child"
d. a trigger-happy war-monger

10. The U.S.-sponsored leader of South Vietnam until his assassination in 1963 was

a. Ngo Dinh Diem
b. Ho Chi Minh
c. Dien Bien Phu
d. Mao Zedong

IV. Fill-in Questions

Fill in each blank in the following statements with the correct information.

1. LBJ's first presidential act was a tax cut of $_____ billion.

2. In 1964, Johnson won _____ percent of the popular vote and majorities in all but six states.

3. As a result of the 1964 election, Democrats had a majority of _____ to _____ in the Senate, and _____ to _____ in the House, the greatest imbalance of power since the _____.

4. By the early 1970s, all southern Democrats were courting _____ voters.

5. Volunteers in Service to America (VISTA) was a domestic _____.

6. The Geneva Accords of 1954 divided Vietnam into two zones pending an election that was to be held after _____ years. (It was never held.)

7. Between 1954 and 1956, about a _____ anti-Communist North Vietnamese fled to South Vietnam. The U.S. established _____ as the leader of South Vietnam and gave him $_____ million in aid just in 1955.

8. The "dominoes" that might topple, according to the "domino theory" proposed by Eisenhower and accepted by later presidents, were Southeast Asian _____.

9. By the end of 1965 there were _____ American soldiers in Vietnam; by the end of 1967 there were _____.

10. In the Tet Offensive, _____ Vietcong and North Vietnamese troops attacked _____ South Vietnamese cities, including Saigon.

11. In 1965, the first year of official combat in Vietnam, the weekly death toll of American soldiers was _____. The following year it was _____ a week, and in 1968, more than _____ died each week.

12. A few weeks after the Tet Offensive, public approval of Johnson's handling of the Vietnam War dropped from ____ percent to ____ percent.

13. About _____ young men left the U.S. to avoid the draft, mostly going to Canada or Sweden, and more than _____ soldiers deserted (almost all briefly).

14. Stokely Carmichael of SNCC expelled _____ from the organization in 1966.

15. According to the National Commission on the Causes and Prevention of Violence, for the period 1963-1968 there were _____ civil rights demonstrations and _____ white terrorist attacks on civil rights workers.

16. Young people, many of them at least nominally part of the counterculture, got "_____" when they went door to door soliciting support for Eugene McCarthy in 1968.

17. George Wallace got _____ percent of the popular vote in 1968.

18. Kevin Phillips predicted (correctly, it turned out) that Republicans would get two-thirds to three-fourths of the _____ vote in 1972.

V. Essay Questions

Write notes under each of the following questions that would help you answer similar essay questions on an exam.

1. Describe the life and background of Lyndon B. Johnson. Was his experience good preparation for the presidency? Why or why not?

2. What steps did Johnson take against segregation? Should Johnson be considered a hero by blacks? Explain.

3. Explain the issues in the 1964 election. Can a landslide like Johnson's be misleading and encourage action against the best judgment of the people? Why or why not?

4. Why was the Voting Rights Act so important to blacks, especially in the South? Was it a useful early step in the 1960s movement to full equality? Explain.

5. What were the elements of the Great Society? Was it misguided or a beneficial effort to end poverty and the plight of the disadvantaged? Explain.

6. What might have been done prior to 1965 to avoid American involvement in Vietnam?

7. What determined who would be a hawk or a dove with regard to the war in Vietnam? Explain.

8. Describe the election of 1968. Who (what groups) supported Nixon, and who supported Humphrey? Why?

9. What facts about the background of the war in Vietnam (before 1960) are important in understanding it?

10. What were the major elements that explain the United States involvement in Vietnam? What were the key turning points? Was it a valiant effort or a catastrophe? Explain.

11. Explain black separatism in contrast to integration. Was black nationalism a viable option blacks in the United States? Why or why not?

12. Describe the student movement and the counterculture to emerge from it. What visible long-term effects did the counterculture have on American life?

13. Describe the antiwar movement. Were the activities of the protesters close to treason or were they symbols of democracy in action? Explain.

14. Examine the quotations under the chapter title. How clearly do the quotations match the policies pursued by the presidents quoted?

ANSWERS

II. True-False

1. True
2. False
3. False
4. True
5. True
6. True
7. True
8. True
9. True
10. True
11. False
12. True
13. False
14. False
15. True
16. True
17. False
18. True
19. False
20. True
21. False
22. False
23. True
24. False
25. True

III. Multiple Choice

1. d
2. b
3. a
4. c
5. b
6. a
7. b
8. b
9. d
10. a

IV. Fill-in

1. $10
2. 61%
3. 68; 32; 295; 140; New Deal
4. African American
5. Peace Corps
6. two
7. million; Ngo Dinh Diem; $320
8. countries
9. 200,000; 500,000
10. 70,000; 30
11. 26; 96; 280
12. 40; 26
13. 40,000; 500,000
14. whites
15. 369; 213
16. "clean for Gene"
17. 13.5%
18. Wallace

49

Presidency in Crisis
The Nixon, Ford, and Carter Administrations
1968-1980

"The superpowers often behave like two heavily armed blind men feeling their way around a room, each believing himself in mortal peril of the other whom he assumes to have perfect vision."

Henry A. Kissinger

"Imagination plays too important a role in the writing of history, and what is imagination but the projection of the author's personality."

Peter Geyl

I. Key Words

You should be able to define the following words and explain their historical significance in relation to the development of American history.

Richard Nixon
"affirmative action"
H. R. Haldeman and John Erlichman
Spiro Agnew
"Silent Majority"
Earl Warren
the Warren Court
Brown v. Board of Education of Topeka (1954)
Roe v. Wade (1973)
Miranda v. Arizona (1968)
Warren Burger
Vietnamization
ARVN
Kent State
Khmer Rouge
Pol Pot
Nguyen Van Thieu
Agent Orange

détente
Henry Kissinger
Realpolitik
Mao Zedong
"playing the China card"
SALT
1973 Yom Kippur War
shuttle diplomacy
Salvador Allende and Augusto Pinochet
"New Age" liberals
Anthony Comstock
"sexual revolution"
AIDS
George McGovern
CREEP
Watergate
the "imperial presidency"
Gerald Ford
25th Amendment
OPEC
WIN!
"stagflation"
Jimmy Carter
Panama Canal treaty
Anwar Sadat
Menachem Begin
Camp David Accords
Zbigniew Brzezinski
Three Mile Island

II. True-False

If the statement is false, change any words necessary to make it true.

1. Public opposition to affirmative action policies probably contributed to the decline of the Democratic party, even though it was Nixon, not Democrats, who reinterpreted affirmative action to become preferential treatment for minorities.

2. Women's voting patterns remained about evenly divided between the two major parties, as had been the case since the 1920s, unaffected by affirmative action.

3. Richard Nixon was just another typical example of a president born to wealth.

4. Nixon repeatedly tried to dismantle New Deal and Great Society social programs.

5. The Warren Court often used contemporary sociological and psychological sources to interpret the meaning of the Constitution, beginning with *Brown v. Board of Education* in 1954.

6. Nixon's strategy for extricating the U.S. from Vietnam was to replace American troops (and casualties) with Vietnamese, as quickly as the ARVN could be retrained and equipped.

7. The policy of "Vietnamization" worked, in that U.S. soldiers were able to leave Vietnam in 1973, but it failed to keep South Vietnam from being overrun by North Vietnam in 1975.

8. The Vietnam War cost the United States more than any other war in our history.

9. Agent Orange was the most habit-forming and dangerous of the dozens of powerful and highly illegal drugs American soldiers brought back from Vietnam.

10. Like his historical idol, Otto von Bismarck, Henry Kissinger believed that a nation's foreign policy ought at all times to reflect the morals and ideals of the nation.

11. Diplomatic contact between China and the United States began with a visit to China by an American Ping-Pong team and led to formal U. S. diplomatic recognition of China in 1979.

12. Kissinger's "shuttle diplomacy" in 1973 helped end the Yom Kippur War.

13. When George McGovern ran for president in 1972 as the Democratic nominee, he could count on support from the traditional sources of Democratic strength—labor unions, big-city political machines, and southern politicians.

14. Nixon's response to the Watergate break-in was to claim that he had personally ordered the burglary for reasons of national security, and that to question his action was "un-American."

15. Vice President Spiro Agnew pleaded no contest to charges that he had accepted bribes when he was governor of Maryland.

16. Gerald Ford became vice-president and then within a year became president due to the resignation of the two men who occupied those offices.

17. Nixon habitually used filthy and bigoted language, even on tape recordings he made of his White House conversations.

18. OPEC justified its big jumps in the price of oil by criticizing Western nations for their irresponsible consumption of cheap energy.

19. Jimmie Carter, despite being virtually unknown outside of Georgia and the South, was in fact an experienced career politician when he ran for the presidency.

20. Anwar Sadat was so angry at Menachem Begin's refusal to compromise that he packed his bags to leave Camp David.

21. Carter's secretary of state was a Polish refugee from Communism and an anti-Soviet ideologue who alienated some of America's allies, but Carter shared (for different reasons) his hostility toward the Soviet Union.

22. By 1979, it was clear that the American response to OPEC's increases in the price of oil was to consume more of it and to import a higher proportion of it, while cutting domestic production.

III. Multiple Choice

1. By the mid-1970s fossil fuels were the source of what percentage of American energy needs?

    a. 30%
    b. 45%
    c. 70%
    d. 90%

2. When President Ford tightened the money supply in order to slow down the economy, it resulted in

    a. a serious recession
    b. a boom in the economy
    c. a decrease in support for Republicans
    d. a reduction in unemployment

3. When television commentators said that there was a bandwagon effect favoring Carter, people responded by

    a. ignoring Carter at campaigns
    b. jumping on the bandwagon
    c. switching to Ford's side
    d. turning off television news

4. Carter had an American way of thinking often described as

a. an illogical emotional viewpoint
b. a view that demands no good evidence
c. intuitive and instinctive
d. an engineer mentality

5. Andrew Young had to resign from the Carter administration because he

a. was black
b. met secretly with the PLO, a terrorist organization
c. was a former civil-rights activist
d. seemed to be alienating black Africa

6. Vice President Spiro Agnew was best known for his fondness for

a. money
b. pizza
c. political in-fighting
d. alliteration in his speeches

7. Nixon and Kissinger believed the Air Force and Navy planes would devastate North Vietnam and force it to

a. surrender
b. the conference table
c. withdraw to the North
d. call upon China for help

8. The Camp David Accords were signed by Israel and

a. Jordan
b. Syria
c. Egypt
d. Palestine

9. Which of these does *not* describe the statistically typical American of 1980?

a. Protestant in religious preference
b. over 30 years of age
c. married (once)
d. Republican in voting preference

10. The major result of Vietnamization was

a. reduction of U.S. casualties in Vietnam
b. ARVN success in defending South Vietnam
c. South Vietnamese military victories in Laos and Cambodia
d. defeat of Ho Chi Minh's forces

11. By 1980, an item that cost 15 cents in 1940 would cost

a. half as much
b. twice as much
c. about the same
d. a dollar

12. "Playing the China card" was an American strategy aimed at

a. North Vietnam
b. South Vietnam
c. the Soviet Union
d. Japan

IV. Fill-in Questions

Fill in each blank in the following statements with the correct information.

1. Grassroots conservatives (whom Nixon called the "_____") were repelled by the social and cultural causes that 1970s liberals embraced, though they tended to be sympathetic toward liberal economic policies.

2. The policy of turning the war over to the ARVN in order to reduce American casualties was called "_____." When Nixon took office in 1969, there were _____ American soldiers in Vietnam. By 1972 there were _____.

3. At Kent State University in Ohio, the National Guard shot _____ students dead and wounded _____. Ten days later, police in Mississippi shot _____ students at Jackson State College.

4. In Cambodia, Pol Pot's followers murdered _____ million people in a population of _____ million.

5. In Vietnam, about _____ million ARVN soldiers were killed; estimates of civilian dead ran as high as _____ million. About _____ percent of the people of Southeast Asia became refugees after the war.

6. The Vietnam War cost the United States $_____ billion, killed _____ Americans and wounded _____.

7. Agent Orange, which turned out to be toxic to persons exposed to it, was intended to be used for _____.

8. In the 1972 election Nixon won _____ percent of the popular vote and carried every state but Massachusetts, a swing of ____ million votes in just eight years.

9. The American divorce rate rose from _____ divorces per 1000 marriages in 1965 to _____ per 1000 marriages in 1979, and the rate of illegitimate births _____ during the 1960s and 1970s.

10. Counting unsuccessful as well as successful attempts, Richard Nixon ran for president _____ times. Eugene Debs ran _____ times, and Norman Thomas (another Socialist) ran _____ times.

11. Nixon resigned the presidency on August 9th, 1974, to avoid _____.

12. By 1973, the U.S., with ____ percent of the world's population, was consuming _____ of the world's annual production of oil.

13. About ____ percent of the oil that Americans consumed in 1973 was produced at home.

14. Ford inherited an inflation rate of ____ percent a year, and it soon rose to ____ percent.

15. By 1980, the annual U.S. inflation rate was nearly ____ percent, and the price of electricity rose by _____ percent.

V. Essay Questions

Write notes under each of the following questions that would help you answer similar essay questions on an exam.

1. Was there a single reason for the crises in the presidencies of Nixon, Ford and Carter, or just an unfortunate series of misfortunes between 1968 and 1980?

2. What were the elements of Nixon's domestic policy? Why do you think he was bored by these issues? Was Nixon really a conservative? Explain with a clear definition of the term.

3. Explain Nixon's Vietnam policy. Was Vietnamization the best policy that the U.S. could have followed under the circumstances? Why?

4. Why did the antiwar movement come to an end so quickly? Was it a fad, a circus, or a serious exercise in democracy? Why?

5. Describe the foreign policy of Kissinger and Nixon. Is it true that only a president with a reputation for being "tough" and anti-Communist could have accomplished what he did? Explain. Was Nixon lucky in foreign policy or insightful and knowledgeable? Give evidence and arguments to support your view.

6. What were the various foreign initiatives of Henry Kissinger? Was he a realist or an idealist in his policy decisions? Why?

7. Describe the election of 1972. What were the major issues in that election?

8. Explain the Watergate scandal. Were the president's actions worth impeachment? Why?

9. Evaluate Gerald Ford's partial term as president. Why was he not reelected in 1976?

10. Explain the energy problems of the United States in the mid-1970s. Will this problem occur again?

11. Describe Jimmy Carter's domestic policies. What were his successes and failures? Were these successes and failures his own doing or the circumstances of time? Explain.

12. What were Jimmy Carter's main foreign policy decisions? What could he have done differently?

13. Examine the statistics relating to the typical American. What are the five most important characteristics of the typical American? Explain why. Do you agree that "the virtue of the United States remains in its diversity of people"? Why or why not?

14. Read the quotations at the beginning of the chapter. How should the nation control the tremendous power of the president? Is a presidential election every four years sufficient? Explain.

ANSWERS

II. True-False

1. True
2. True
3. False
4. False
5. True
6. True
7. True
8. False
9. False
10. False
11. True
12. True
13. False
14. False
15. True
16. True
17. True
18. True
19. False
20. True
21. True
22. True

III. Multiple Choice

1. d
2. a
3. b
4. d
5. b
6. d
7. b
8. c
9. d
10. a
11. d
12. c

III. Fill-in

1. "silent majority"
2. "Vietnamization"; 541,000; 24,000
3. 4; 11; 2
4. 3; 7.2
5. 1; 3.5; 10%
6. $150; 57,000; 300,000
7. defoliation
8. 60.8; 20
9. 2.5; 5.3; tripled
10. 3; 5; 6
11. impeachment
12. 6%; one-third
13. 61%
14. 9%; 12%
15. 20%; 200%

50

Morning in America
The Age of Reagan, 1980-1993

"Carter believes fifty things, but no one thing."

"the Great Communicator, Ronald Reagan."

"History is the sextant and compass of states, which, tossed by wind and current, would be lost in confusion if they could not fix their position."

Alan Nevins

I. Key Words

You should be able to define the following words and explain their historical significance in relation to the development of American history.

mullahs
Ayatollah Ruhollah Khomeini
Ronald Reagan
political action committees (PACs)
the "Reagan Revolution" and "the Teflon president"
"Just Say No!"
Reaganomics
"supply-side economics"
"sagebrush rebels"
Federal Savings and Loan Insurance Corporation (FSLIC)
"junk bonds"
"sleaze factor"
"Morning in America"
the "evil empire"
Muammar Qadaffi
Grenada
Sandinistas
Iran-Contra affair
Oliver North
Strategic Defense Initiative (SDI) ("Star Wars")
Mikhail Gorbachev
perestroika and *glasnost*

Michael Dukakis
George Bush
Tiananmen Square massacre
Boris Yeltsin
Gulf War
Saddam Hussein
"Vietnam Syndrome"
Bill Clinton
H. Ross Perot

II.   True-False

If the statement is false, change any words necessary to make it true.

1. Weapons systems developed during the Carter administration proved to be keys to victory in the Gulf War against Iraq.

2. Reagan refused to support rebels in Afghanistan who were fighting Soviet troops.

3. Colonel Oliver North refused to sell Hawk missiles to Iran.

4. In 1986 Reagan won applause by bombing Libya.

5. Reagan presented himself as a born-again Christian on a mission from God.

6. Carter admitted the Shah of Iran to the United States for medical treatment, but Khomeini did not respond.

7. By 1989, the year Reagan left office, the richest 1 percent owned 48 percent of the nation's wealth.

8. When Reagan celebrated his seventy-eighth birthday in 1989, he became the third oldest man ever to be president.

9. Rather more remarkable than good luck was Ronald Reagan's immunity from blame for his blunders.

10. While Reagan called for a constitutional amendment to obligate Congress to balance the budget, he annually approved budgets that sent the deficit and the national debt soaring to record heights.

11. The "sagebrush rebels" were western conservationists who wanted to control the exploitation of public lands by mining, logging and cattle companies.

12. Ronald Reagan was impeached (but not convicted) for violating the Boland Amendment.

III. Multiple Choice

1. In the election of 1992, Ross Perot

   a. tried to become Bush's vice-presidential candidate
   b. advocated an end to primary elections
   c. quit the race and then, later, jumped back in
   d. helped the Republican campaign

2. After rioting broke out against Marcos in the Philippines, the United States

   a. gave full support to the dictator
   b. stayed out of the incident
   c. played a central role in his ouster
   d. sent in American troops

3. The most controversial of Reign's weapons proposals was SDI, which

   a. prepared the United States for a first-strike nuclear attack
   b. would attempt to create an anti-missile system to prevent a missile attack
   c. would cost less than an increase in missiles
   d. was approved by the Soviet Union

4. The "supply-side" theory of economist Arthur Laffler called for

   a. higher taxes on the wealthy
   b. high tariffs and trade restrictions
   c. liberal spending on social services
   d. increasing the nation's supply of goods and services

5. Reagan was known as "the Teflon president" because

   a. he invested heavily in related companies
   b. nothing messy stuck to him
   c. he was tough in a crisis
   d. he used the word in his speeches

6. In the election of 1988, Michael Dukakis

   a. denied his membership in the ACLU
   b. defended the parole policies in Massachusetts
   c. explained his disagreements with many ACLU policies
   d. called for a "kinder, gentler, America."

7. Communist hard-liners in China

a. succeeded in holding onto power in China
b. gave in to the Tiananmen Square students
c. declared war on Tibet
d. cut off communications with the West

8. The Gulf War was precipitated by the invasion of

a. Iraq
b. Kuwait
c. Saudi Arabia
d. Iran

9. The collapse of the "evil empire" came during the administration of Soviet Premier

a. Gorbachev
b. Yeltsin
c. Ceausescu
d. Honecker

10. "Just Say No!" was the slogan Nancy Reagan used to oppose

a. unpopular Supreme Court decisions
b. "supply-side" economics
c. illegal drug use
d. inflation

IV. Fill-in Questions

Fill in each blank in the following statements with the correct information.

1. A typical family making $75,000 paid _____ percent in income tax in the 1950s, but by 1985 paid _____ percent.

2. In 1992 Clinton won _____ percent of the popular vote.

3. In 1987 the Soviets destroyed _____ missiles and the Americans _____.

4. The Defense Department paid General Dynamics $_____ for an alignment pin that cost _____ in a hardware store.

5. The Reagan administration spent $_____ on old and new weapons systems.

6. By 1981, the federal government owed $_____ billion, about ____ cents on every dollar produced or earned in the U.S. that year. Eight years later, at the end of the Reagan administration, the national debt was $_____ trillion, or ____ cents on every dollar produced and earned.

7. In one year, Michael Milken collected $_____ in commissions.

8. Government revenues dropped by $_____ during Reagan's time in office.

9. Ross Perot won _____ percent of the popular vote in 1992.

10. In 1983, the United States spent _____ per capita on public broadcasting, as compared to $_____ per capita in Japan, $_____ in Great Britain, and $_____ in Canada.

11. The B-1 bomber of the Reagan Administration was a $_____ billion flop.

12. By 1985, the U.S. and the Soviet Union had more than ____ nuclear warheads between them.

13. The Russian word for "restructuring" the Soviet economy was _____.

14. George Bush ordered a halt to the ground war in Iraq when the war was _____ hours old.

V. Essay Questions

Write notes under each of the following questions that would help you answer similar essay questions on an exam.

1. Evaluate the efforts at disarmament made during the Reagan administration. Was Reagan overly cautious? Why or why not?

2. Using statistical data, argue that the American people, as a whole, were better off in 1992 than in 1980. Now make a case for the opposite view. Can you use the same data for each side of the debate?

3. Describe the financial frauds of the 1980s. Is this problem to be expected in a free-enterprise system, or was it unusual and excessive? To what extent were the Reagan administration's attitudes or policies responsible?

4. How could Carter be so successful at Camp David and yet fail in the hostage crisis? What were the differences between the two events?

5. Evaluate Ronald Reagan as president. What were his strengths and his weaknesses? Be specific.

6. Compare the election of 1988 with that of 1992. Why did George Bush win in 1988 and lose in 1992?

7. Explain why the liberals lost their majority in Congress following the 1980s. Does the affluence of American society tend against liberalism? Explain.

8. Explain the ideas of Reaganomics. Explain the "supply-side" concept.

9. Describe the troubles Reagan had with his appointees. Why did he survive the unpopular behavior of some of these subordinates?

10. Describe the crisis in the Middle East and the "Hundred Hours War." Were the results worth the cost? Explain.

11. What were the three major foreign policy decisions of Ronald Reagan? Explain each.

ANSWERS

II. True-False

1. True
2. False
3. False
4. True
5. True
6. False
7. True
8. False
9. True
10. True
11. False
12. False

III. Multiple Choice

1. c
2. c
3. b
4. d
5. b
6. c
7. a
8. b
9. a
10. c

IV. Fill-in

1. 52.9; 29.6
2. 43
3. 1,752; 867
4. $7,417; 3 cents
5. $2 trillion
6. 738; 26; 2.1; 43
7. $550 million
8. $131 billion
9. 19
10. 57 cents; $10; $18; $22
11. $30
12. 50,000
13. *perestroika*
14. 100

51

The Millennium Years
Decadence? Renewal?
1993-2003

"Sex, violence, mudslinging. Americans love it. Always have. It's democracy. It's not always nice."

Sean Cosgrove

"America is the last best hope of the world."

Abraham Lincoln

I. Key Words

You should be able to define the following words and explain their historical significance in relation to the development of American history.

"decadence"
cults
Unification Church
"Moonies"
"New Age"
"political correctness" (PC)
Rush Limbaugh
the occult right
Timothy McVeigh
Janet Reno
Bill Clinton
"New Democrats"
Somalia
Haiti
Jean-Bertrand Aristide
Bosnia-Herzegovina
Bosnian Serbs, Croatians, and Muslims
Kosovo
Slobodan Milosevich
"ethnic cleansing"
North American Free Trade Agreement (NAFTA)
"U.S. English" lobby

health care reform
the "Solid South"
Newt Gingrich
"Republican revolution"
1994 mid-term election
Kevin Phillips
"don't ask, don't tell"
American Association of Retired Persons (AARP)
Robert Dole
cyber-America
"dot-coms"
Monica Lewinsky
Kenneth Starr
Starr report
Al Gore
John McCain
George W. Bush ("W")
9-11-2001
al Qaeda
Osama bin Laden
Taliban
Saddam Hussein
Second Iraq War
Kyoto global warming treaty
Enron

II.   True-False

If the statement is false, change any words necessary to make it true.

1. Nearly half of the century's last seven presidents blatantly broke the law.

2. Predictions made at the close of a century are notoriously inaccurate. According to the *Ladies Home Journal* in 1900, by the year 2000, the second most widely spoken language in the United States would be Russian, and the American population would be half a billion.

3. In the "New Age," according to the text, most popular religious cults were based on well-founded (and Western) philosophies long recognized as part of Christian faiths.

4. "New Age" fads in the 1980s and 1990s had their roots in the 1960s hippie counterculture.

5. Though the New Age was not political, the mentality it encouraged shaped American culture as the religious cults did not.

6. The term *politically correct* originated among 1930s and 1940s Communists, but the "PC" sentiments of the 20th century's latter decades had little to do with the American Communist party, which was essentially dead by 1970.

7. Left-leaning political correctness, found mostly in the nation's universities, had a mirror image on the far right of the political spectrum, whose spokesmen could be found primarily on AM "talk radio."

8. The bombing of the Murrah Federal Building in Oklahoma City in 1995 was in retaliation for the raid by federal agents on a religious compound in Waco, Texas, on the same day two years earlier.

9. Until her abrupt removal in Clinton's first term, Janet Reno was the first woman to serve as attorney general, one of the top four cabinet positions.

10. Bill Clinton's wife, Hillary Rodham, had been a Republican in her youth.

11. Though he used the term "New Democrat" to call attention to his domestic policies, Bill Clinton was first and foremost a foreign policy-oriented president when he took office.

12. Congress passed the NAFTA legislation over Clinton's veto.

13. Mexico became the nation's biggest trading partner after NAFTA was signed.

14. The greatest influx of immigrants to the U.S. in recent years came from the Balkans and other European regions threatened by religious rivalries, "ethnic cleansing," and extreme poverty.

15. The greatest stress of the late-century immigration was language, though a majority of Spanish-speaking and Asian immigrants wanted their children to be educated exclusively in English.

16. Bill Clinton was the most frugal president since Calvin Coolidge, and in several years of his presidency, the government collected more revenue than it spent (reducing the national debt.)

17. The "Solid South" voted consistently Democratic between 1880 and 1944 primarily because of race, since the national Democratic party supported white supremacy in the South.

18. Beginning in 1968, working- and middle-class white voters came to see the Democratic party as the party of minorities and outlandish causes—feminism, abortion on demand, gay rights and other "lifestyle" issues.

19. New Gingrich bragged about a "Republican revolution," but he knew better than to alienate voters dependent on Social Security by cutting their benefits.

20. The president of a major computer manufacturer said in 1977 that "there is no reason anyone would want a computer in their home."

21. The women's movement lost all credibility, according to the text, by siding with Monica Lewinsky, rather than the president, in the Clinton sex scandal.

22. "Dubya's" SAT scores were higher than Bill Clinton's, but George W. Bush appeared to be not very bright.

23. The outcome of the 2000 election was essentially decided by a 5-4 vote in the Supreme Court.

24. Following the attacks on the World Trade Center and the Pentagon, American Muslims reported an upsurge in violent personal attacks on Arab-Americans and others who looked as if they might be Muslim. Seven lynchings were reported.

25. The stock market peaked in March 2000 and then collapsed because of the bursting of the "high-tech" bubble ("dot-coms" that had been overvalued.)

III. Multiple Choice

1. The intervention of American troops in Somalia

   a. failed as a humanitarian mission
   b. took place with United Nations approval
   c. ended the civil war there
   d. was in cooperation with General Aidid

2. The Bosnian Muslims

   a. were the chief sufferers in Bosnia
   b. received aid from the Croats
   c. finally achieved victory in 1995
   d. joined American troops to attack Macedonia

3. The Democrats were losing traditional supporters because

   a. they approved low tariffs
   b. they reached out to racial, ethnic, and lifestyle minorities
   c. they favored states' rights
   d. they rejected affirmative action

4. By 1999, American ground troops were occupying

a. Bosnia
b. Mexico
c. Somalia
d. all of these

5. Clinton's biggest political setback was his plan for

a. NAFTA
b. NASA
c. national health insurance
d. balancing the federal budget

6. By 1989, the African nation of Somalia

a. was a Soviet pawn
b. was the site of American Cold War military bases
c. was an example of African development and political stability
d. was of no importance to the U.S. strategic outlook

7. The pattern for NAFTA was

a. the European Community
b. NATO
c. the United Nations
d. the Great Society

8. The "Republican Revolution" led by Newt Gingrich lasted until

a. the defeat of NAFTA
b. 1995, when Congress shut down the government by failing to pass a budget
c. 1994, when Democrats gained control of Congress and kept it
d. the present

9. According to Jacques Barzun, American civilization was "decadent" because

a. institutions function painfully
b. boredom and fatigue are great historical forces
c. society is particularly restless, seeing no clear line of advance
d. all of these

10. According to the text, "political correctness" in American universities and elsewhere was similar to

   a. 1950s anti-Communist McCarthyism
   b. 1930s Communism
   c. the historical method (making judgments on the basis of evidence)
   d. mental illness

IV. Fill-in Questions

Fill in each blank in the following statements with the correct information.

1. When federal agents besieged, then stormed the Branch Davidians' compound in Waco, Texas, in 1993, _____ people were killed, including _____ children.

2. The bombing of the federal building in Oklahoma City killed _____.

3. Bill Clinton was just _____ years old when he was elected governor of Arkansas in 1978.

4. NAFTA provided for the elimination, over a period of _____ years, of trade barriers among _____, the _____, and _____.

5. The leading trading partner of the United States is _____.

6. _____ percent of all so-called "Japanese" cars sold in the United States actually were manufactured in the United States by American workers.

7. The greatest influx of immigrants to the U.S. in the final decades of the 20th century was from _____.

8. The annual per capita expenditure on medical care in the U.S. during the 1990s was $_____; in Switzerland, the second most expensive country, the amount was $_____.

9. In 1993, _____ million Americans had no health insurance.

10. Profits in the pharmaceutical industry were often more than _____ percent.

11. Between 1983 and 1998 the number of health-care managers increased by _____ percent, while the number of doctors increased by _____ percent.

12. In recent years, fewer than _____ percent of black voters vote Republican.

13. After 1968, the only elections in which the Democratic party was able to win enough white votes in the South to carry southern states was then the party nominated a _____ to run for president.

14. Within a year of the 1994 election _____ Democratic officeholders switched to the Republican party.

15. During Clinton's presidency, the earnings of the poorest fifth of the population rose by _____ percent, while the income of the richest fifth climbed by _____ percent.

16. The unspoken U.S. military policy regarding homosexuality was always "_____."

17. The Whitewater investigation of the Clintons cost $_____ million.

18. Clinton won reelection in 1996 by an electoral vote of _____ to _____, but the Democrats failed to gain control of _____.

19. On an average day in 1996, _____ Americans were born, (to mothers _____ percent of whom were not married), and _____ Americans died; _____ people got married, but _____ got divorced.

20. _____ percent of American households were on the Internet in 1996, _____ percent two years later, and _____ percent by 2001. As early as 1977, IBM had sold _____ "personal computers."

21. "Dubya" raised $_____ million for the 2000 election campaign.

22. In the 9-11 attack, _____ people died, including _____ firefighters and _____ police officers.

V. Essay Questions

Write notes under each of the following questions that would help you answer similar essay questions on an examination.

1. Explain what the Clinton administration was trying to accomplish in Somalia and Haiti.

2. What were the arguments for and against NAFTA? Why would a trade agreement become so controversial? What other data would help you understand the issues surrounding NAFTA?

3. Why did Clinton's health care program fail? What political lessons might be learned from its failure?

4. Describe the sexual revolution. What moral issues arise out of this movement?

5. What were the main issues involved with the women's movement? Explain each issue.

6. What made the policy of affirmative action controversial? Explain the arguments for and against this policy. Be sure you have a clear definition of what the policy means.

7. Why did the Republicans win control of Congress in 1994? What evidence is there to support an argument that the American people may prefer to have one party control the presidency and the other control Congress?

8. Should a definition of "decadence" include rampant greed?

9. Discuss the quote by John Gardner at the beginning of the chapter. In what ways might this observation apply to the description of events in this chapter?

10. Was Clinton's moral goal for foreign policy realistic? Does it necessarily involve the United States playing "policeman to the world?" Explain.

ANSWERS

II. True-False

1. True
2. True
3. False
4. True
5. True
6. True
7. True
8. True
9. False
10. True
11. False
12. False
13. False
14. False
15. True
16. True
17. True
18. True
19. False
20. True
21. False
22. True
23. True
24. False
25. True

III. Multiple Choice

1. b
2. a
3. b
4. a
5. c
6. d
7. a
8. b
9. d
10. a

IV. Fill-in

1. 80; 20
2. 168
3. 32
4. 15; Canada, United States; Mexico
5. Canada
6. 40%
7. Mexico
8. $3,700; $2,644
9. 39
10. 1000%
11. 683%; 50%
12. 10%
13. southerner
14. 137
15. 1%; 15%
16. "don't ask, don't tell"
17. $50
18. 379; 159; Congress
19. 11,000; 31%; 6,000; 7,000; 3,000
20. 9%; 20%; 50%; 25,000
21. $60
22. 2,801; 343; 75